And Now You Know

And Now You Know

The Rest of the Story from the Lives of Well-Known Latter-day Saints

LARRY E. MORRIS

EAGLE
GATE

To Isaac, Courtney, Justin, and Whitney

Library of Congress Cataloging-in-Publication Data

Morris, Larry E., 1951–
    And now you know / Larry E. Morris.
        p.   cm.
    ISBN 1-57008-827-6 (alk. paper)
    1. Mormons—United States—Biography.   I. Title.

BX8693.M67 2002
289.3'092'2—dc21   2002001715

Printed in the United States of America   72076-6954
Publishers Printing, Salt Lake City, UT

10   9   8   7   6   5   4   3   2   1

CONTENTS

Led by the Spirit: Modern Miracles

AGAINST ALL ODDS:
COURAGE IN THE FACE OF
ADVERSITY AND PERSECUTION

A YOUNG BOY
LOSES HIS SIGHT

W
hen he was fifteen years old, a thoughtful young man recorded a tragic accident in which he was involved four years earlier:

"On October 10, 1873, while working after nightfall—a very dark night—a fearful accident occurred. My brother Albert, then about six years of age, came quietly towards me as I was still working with a digging fork in my hands; he gave no notice of his approach and until he screamed I had not an idea he was near me; then to my horror I discovered that while in the act of pitching with the fork I had struck him with the tool, one grain piercing the ball of his left eye. This organ was finally entirely removed, though not before the right eye had become sympathetically affected and he was almost entirely blind, being only enabled to distinguish very bright colors, and then only when within a few inches of the eye. . . . I need say nothing in regard to my feelings and reflections at this mishap; but that my relief lies in the promise pronounced on him by the priesthood of God that he shall recover."

The brothers were third-generation members of the Church because their grandfather and father had both converted to Mormonism. Three years after the accident, the family gathered to Zion, settling in Provo, Utah. At that time, schools for the blind were rare and had not been established anywhere in the state, but Albert obtained fifteen or twenty books in line-letter and taught himself how to read. Many years later, a school for the blind was founded in Ogden, and at thirty years of age, Albert became one of the first students. There he met and fell in love with Sarah Whalen, a teacher at the school. They were married in the Salt Lake Temple a few days before Christmas in 1905.

Rather than having his sight restored, Albert's blessing was to bless the lives of other blind individuals. At Brigham Young Academy he studied various occupations for the blind, such as hammock making, chair caning, reed weaving, and basket making. He also became an expert typist. He then returned to teach at the Odgen school for the blind. During this time, he was continually thinking of ways he could help blind members of the Church, who had virtually no access to the vast storehouse of printed Church literature. Albert and Sarah visited blind people throughout Utah and taught many of them to read Braille.

In 1903, with the help of Weber Stake Academy president David O. McKay, Albert spearheaded an effort to raise seven hundred dollars—an enormous sum at the time—purchased a press, and began printing reading material for the blind. A year later, under the direction of Church president Joseph F. Smith, Albert helped found the Society for Aid of the Sightless, serving as manager with his wife, Sarah, as secretary. Together, they began printing missionary tracts and other Church literature in Braille, making them available to both Church members and investigators for the first time.

Printing in Braille was a complicated process that involved inserting brass plates, imprinting dots by pushing the appropriate keys and pressing a foot lever, printing the letters from the plates to twenty-two-inch by twelve-inch sheets of paper, folding the sheets, hanging them on racks to dry, and finally stapling them together and packing them in cartons for mailing. When Albert obtained his first press, it ran too fast to allow a blind operator to insert and remove sheets of paper. Although experts were unable to solve the problem, Albert set up a foot lever that allowed him to apply a brake and at the same time pull the motor away from the drive wheel. He was thus able to run the press at a desired speed and still stop it immediately if necessary.

Albert's ingenuity manifested itself in a number of other interesting ways. Since he and Sarah frequently visited blind people in other parts of the state, they needed to make sure their chickens were fed while they were gone. Albert devised an ingenious device that caused a feed bag to automatically open when an alarm clock rang. The chickens soon learned the meaning of the alarm and would scamper toward it whenever it rang.

Albert was also an expert gardener, and he invented a small greenhouse—complete with windows, an electricity source, a light bulb, a lever, and tubes of mercury. The windows were designed to automatically close or open, depending on the temperature. The uniform heat allowed Albert to prepare young plants for transplanting in three weeks time. His garden was said to be full of glorious plants and flowers from early spring to late fall.

In 1912, Albert and Sarah began publishing *The Messenger to the Sightless*, a Braille magazine containing Church literature and doctrine, articles, poems, general conference addresses, and other items of interest. It was sent free of charge to blind people throughout the world. Albert ran the press from his home and published *The Messenger to the Sightless* every month for more than forty years—an incredible length of time—until his retirement in 1953 at the age of eighty-six. His wife, Sarah, was his partner in this effort until she died in 1942.

His older brother was devastated by the accident that took Albert's sight, and his biographer speculated that it possibly accounted for his "deep, almost fanatical dedication to work, to Church duties and to all the serious adult responsibilities" that marked his life from that time forward. But the Lord had a plan for this sorrowful young man. In 1911, at the age of forty-nine, he was called to the Quorum of the Twelve.

The brothers, James Edward Talmage and Albert Mansell Talmage, were both born in Hungerford, England. James, born on 21 September 1862, was fourteen years old when the family emigrated to Utah. Albert, born on 15 October 1867, was nine. Young James enrolled at Brigham Young Academy and was soon at the top of his class. He was befriended by academy principal Karl G. Maeser (then in his early 50s), who recognized the young man's unique potential for learning. By the time he was seventeen, James was teaching physiology, Latin, and shorthand at the academy.

At Brother Maeser's encouragement—and after a personal interview in which Church president John Taylor approved his plans—James furthered his quest for learning at Lehigh University in Bethlehem, Pennsylvania, and Johns Hopkins University in Baltimore, Maryland, both highly prestigious universities. He excelled in chemistry and geology. Although he spent only one year at Lehigh, for example, he was awarded credit for freshman, sophomore, junior, and senior classes in such subjects as qualitative analysis, organic chemistry, and medical chemistry. He frequently complemented his classroom work with field trips and laboratory experiments. Then, in 1888, after James had returned to Provo, his empathy for Albert's blindness took on increased depth when a laboratory accident threatened his own sight.

On 20 February, not long after celebrating his election to the Provo City Council, James was pouring molten slag into a mold when some of the molten material exploded and penetrated his left eye. He immediately obtained what first aid he could and had both eyes bandaged. Then, despite intense, searing pain, he attended a city council meeting as a blind man and was sworn to his new position as councilman on the very evening of the accident.

For weeks, James endured continual pain and an uncertain future, his worries no doubt compounded by haunting memories of the accident involving his brother Albert. He moved from his bachelor apartment into the home of Sister Josiah Cluff, who cared for him during this period. Fortunately, with the aid of regular medical treatment and priesthood blessings, his sight returned in full by the early part of March.

In 1891, three years after his marriage to Mary May Booth, James returned to England to attend meetings of the Royal Microscopical Society and to obtain family records for temple work. During this trip, he was able to visit the area where he and Albert had grown up. "Among other desires," he wrote with a touch of humor, "I have longed to go a-fishing again, *as I used to do*, in the Canal that passes through the town. Today, Elder Pyre and myself prepared for this species of recreation. I fully realized the wish expressed above—fished *as I used to do*, staying hour after hour at the water side, and catching nothing."

James served as president of the Society for Aid of the Sightless and (probably accompanied by Albert) met Helen Keller when she came to Salt Lake City. Inspired by her example, the two brothers worked hand-in-hand to improve the quality of life for blind members of the Church. After his call to the Twelve, James spoke at a conference in Cache Valley, Utah. After the meeting, a blind woman introduced herself and said that she wished very much to read *The Messenger to the Sightless* but lacked the keen sense of touch required to read Braille. When James reported this conversation to his brother, Albert sent the woman Braille lessons that used extra large dots, enabling her to learn Braille and soon read the magazine.

James, of course, is best remembered for his powerful theological works *The Articles of Faith* and *Jesus the Christ*, both among the few works published under the name of the Church. These books, written

in his elegant, clear style, have strengthened the testimonies of count-
less individuals, as well as having a significant impact on Church doctrine. James was also blessed to return to his homeland of England to
serve as president of the European Mission from 1924 to 1928.

Although James was just five years older than Albert, he preceded
Albert in death by more than twenty years, dying suddenly of a strep-
tococcus infection in 1933. He was seventy years old. His headstone
in the Salt Lake City Cemetery offers a fitting memoriam to this
uniquely gifted individual:

> JAMES E. TALMAGE
> 1862-1933
> EDUCATOR-SCIENTIST-APOSTLE
> *"Within the gospel of Jesus Christ*
> *there is room and place for every truth*
> *thus far learned by man,*
> *or yet to be made known." J. E. T.*

Just four short months before Albert's death in 1954, the
Improvement Era published a tribute to Albert by Irene M. Jones that
aptly summed up his life of service: "Albert Talmage characterized his
work with and for the blind as 'a mission' and because of this he has
met and overcome many trials and tribulations which would have
brought a less valiant spirit down to defeat and despair. Now, in his
eighty-seventh year, there is about him that surprising gentleness, that
mellowness that so often accompanies age. We recognize in him the
urge to continue individual existence no matter what his infirmities
may be, and to approach the end of his own personal drama with
grace, balance, and wisdom. We are grateful that God placed him here
among us and touched his soul with kindness, nobility, and gentleness."

"My Dear Zina Passed to Her Final Rest"

When he was forty-four years old, a well-known orator and writer endured the loss of his wife Zina. She left one-year-old twins, Paul and Virginia. "For many years," he later wrote, "Zina had suffered from an internal ailment which caused her at times great agony. . . . Occasionally, on coming home, I would find her stretched out upon the floor, unconscious, her teeth set and her fingers tightly clenched in the palms of her hands, showing the terrible torture that she had undergone. . . . Finally an operation was determined on."

Zina returned home after several weeks in the hospital, the operation offering only temporary relief. Despite her suffering, Zina wanted to be with her family, which included six other children besides the twin babies. She also did her best to carry on with other activities. "There was a banquet," wrote her husband, " . . . and Zina, by request, contributed a humorous recitation, much enjoyed by all. That was the last time she and I were out together.

"Spring came, and one morning, after a night of dreadful suffering, she went to the Temple, Fanny Clayton taking her in a carriage and bringing her home after she had been blessed. She took to her bed and never again rose. On the twentieth of May, in her forty-second year—the twenty-first of our married life—my dear Zina passed to her final rest.

"The funeral, in accordance with her often-expressed desire, was held in the home, President Joseph F. Smith and President George Q. Cannon being the principal speakers. The others were Brigham S. Young and James E. Talmage. President Snow was also there, but did not speak."

Reliving these memories, Orson F. Whitney recalled a poignant, moving scene involving the motherless twins: "At the conclusion of the service and while the funeral cortege was forming, a most pathetic incident occurred. From an upstairs window, little Paul and Virginia, in their nurse's arms, looked out in wonderment upon the scene below, waving tiny hands and laughing in childish glee as the casket containing their mother's body was borne to the waiting hearse. Poor little innocents! How could they know what was taking place!"

At the funeral, President Cannon had said of the twins that providence would watch over them. This promise was fulfilled when May Minerva Wells, whom Orson married nine years after marrying Zina, "consented to take charge of the entire household and do a mother's part by all my children; the youngest—the twins—then but one and a half years old. . . . She dismissed the hired help—so indispensable during Zina's illness and for some time after her death—and took upon herself all the cares of housekeeping with such small assistance as my little daughters were able to render."

In his poetic way, Orson recorded that the twins "lived and throve, by the blessing of God, in the tender care of one who loved them as her own." They both lived to adulthood. Paul may have inherited some of his mother Zina's health problems, for he also died in his early forties, in 1942. Virginia, however, lived a long, full life, dying in 1984 at age eighty-five.

A gifted speaker, writer, poet, educator, and spiritual leader, Orson F. Whitney was a true Renaissance man. The grandson of both Heber C. Kimball and Newell K. Whitney, he served as bishop of the Salt Lake Eighteenth Ward for twenty-eight years before his call to the Quorum of the Twelve at age fifty. He died in 1931, four years before his second wife, May.

"Every Heart Is Filled with Sorrow"

J oseph and Hyrum Smith were martyred at Carthage Jail a few minutes after 5:00 on Thursday afternoon, 27 June 1844. The next
morning, Willard Richards—who had survived the violence at
Carthage with a slight graze—Samuel Smith, younger brother of
Joseph and Hyrum, and friend Artois Hamilton placed the bodies of
the two slain prophets in separate wagons and covered them with
branches to protect them from the sun. They left Carthage about 8:00
in the morning and about seven hours later reached Nauvoo, where
they were met by a large gathering of grieving Saints.

Two days later, a woman who witnessed these tragic events wrote
the following letter to her husband, then campaigning in the East for
Joseph Smith's candidacy for United States president. The letter offers
a dramatic picture of how the martyrdom affected the faithful Saints
and what life was like in Nauvoo during those tumultuous days.

> Nauvoo
>
> 30 June 1844
>
> My Dear Companion
>
> Never before, did I take up my pen to address you under
> so trying circumstances as we are now placed, but as Br
> [George] Adams the bearer of this can tell you more than I
> can write I shall not attempt to discribe the scene that we
> have passed through. God forbid that I should ever witness
> another like unto it. I saw the lifeless corpes of our beloved
> brethren when they were brought to their almost distracted

families. Yea I witnessed their tears, and groans, which was enough to rend the heart of an adamant, every brother and sister that witnessed the scene felt deeply to simpathyse with them. Yea, every heart is filled with sorrow, and the very streets of Nauvoo seam to morn. Where it will end the Lord only knows.

We are kept awake night after night by the alarm of mobs. These apostates say, their damnation is sealed, their die is cast, their doom is fixed and they are determined to do all in their power to have revenge. [William] Law says he wants nine more, that was in his quorum [of the Twelve]. Some time I am afraid he will get them. I have no doubt but you are one. What makes me feer, is from a circumstance that took place where the legeon was first called out to defend the city. There was several drums found with blood on, no one could account for it . . . but I try to submit all things into the hands of God.

I have felt aposed their sending for you to come home at present and didnot know as they would untill brother Adams called her a few minutes ago, and told me he should start in about too hours, if I wanted to write I must send it to the mantion house within that time. So I have not time to say much, neither is it nesaceray as he can tell you all, my helth is geting better, the children are well. I mailed a letter to you last monday directed to Baltimore. The letters you sent from Washington all came to gather last wednesday, and a paper, the mail has not ben in before for fore weeks. The letter you sent from Pitsburg I have never got. When I red your pressing invitation for me to meet you, and that you had got a witness that I should do so, I again took courage that some door would open that I should yet go. But Alass my hopes are all blasted.

My constent prayer now is, for the Lord to presurve us all to meet again. I have no doubt but your life will be sought, but may the Lord give you wisdom, to escape their hands. My time is up to send this, so you must excuse me for I have writen in a great hurry and with a bad pen. The children all remember you in love. Now fare you well my love till we meet, which may the Lord grant for his sons sake. Amen.

Like the estimated ten thousand other mourners in Nauvoo, this sister and her children filed past the bodies of Joseph and Hyrum as they lay in state in the dining room of the Mansion House. "To look upon the noble, lifeless forms . . . ," Eliza R. Snow later wrote, "was a sight that might well appal the heart of a true American citizen; but what it was for loving wives and children, the loyal heart may *feel*." At the public funeral, the closed caskets were actually filled with sand, so that bounty hunters could not find the bodies, which were secretly buried in the basement of the Nauvoo House.

The shock and grief that settled over Nauvoo had hardly abated when tragedy struck again: Samuel Smith, who had contracted a fever while fleeing mobbers the night of the martyrdom, died a month later, on 30 July. A witness to the Book of Mormon and one of the first missionaries of the restored gospel, Samuel was only thirty-six when he died. He left a wife and seven children and—like Joseph and Hyrum—was survived by his mother, Lucy Mack Smith, who had now witnessed the deaths of six of her seven sons.

Five weeks after writing the above letter, the sister was reunited with her husband, who arrived from the East with several other members of the Twelve on 6 August. They traveled by stagecoach, boat, and buggy, reaching Nauvoo forty days after the martyrdom and "were received with joy by our families and friends."

Before receiving the letter from his wife, Vilate Murray Kimball, Heber C. Kimball had experienced premonitions of the Prophet's death. As recorded in the *History of the Church*, "Elders Heber C. Kimball and Lyman Wight traveled from Philadelphia to New York by railway and steamboat. Elder Kimball felt very mournful as though he had lost some friend, and knew not the cause."

Still recovering from their own sorrow over Joseph and Hyrum's deaths, Heber and fellow apostles Brigham Young, Orson Pratt, Wilford Woodruff, and Lyman Wight arrived in Nauvoo and found that the Saints "felt like sheep without a shepherd." A few days later, when Sidney Rigdon and Brigham Young both addressed a large gathering of five thousand Church members, Sidney expressed his desire to be the guardian of the Church. His speech aroused little passion, but when Brigham spoke, several in the congregation saw the mantle of Joseph fall upon him.

Fifteen-year-old George Q. Cannon wrote that "it was the voice of Joseph himself; and not only was it the voice of Joseph which was heard, but it seemed in the eyes of the people as though it was the very person of Joseph which stood before them." Heber—Brigham's cousin and best friend—and Vilate voted with virtually the entire congregation to have the Church led by the Twelve.

Heber and Vilate, his first wife, had the blessing of being among a small group of Saints who received the temple ordinances from Joseph Smith before the Nauvoo Temple was completed. When the temple was ready, Elizabeth Ann Whitney, Mary Ann Young, and Vilate were the first to perform initiatory rites. Vilate, faithful throughout her life, died in October of 1867, and her stalwart husband, Heber, exactly eight months later.

A Son Taken
in His Youth

On a sunny day in August of 1932, two brothers fifteen and fourteen years old went surfing at Santa Monica Beach in Southern California. Suddenly one end of the older brother's surfboard caught in the sand and the other end struck him in the stomach. He suffered internal hemorrhaging and started to cough up blood.

The young man was rushed to the hospital, where his parents and other family members soon gathered. They spent a sleepless night as doctors gave the boy blood transfusions and operated in an attempt to stop the bleeding. The next day, however, a blood clot formed and caused the young man's death. The parents were heartbroken at the death of their eldest son. They had also lost a two-year-old daughter fifteen years earlier.

The young man's father, a stake president who had formerly served as a mission president in Europe, wrote that his son was "free from vice and meanness of every kind, and so considerate of his parents. He loved the gospel and had a fine voice with which to defend it. He and his mother were such pals that it will take a long time for her to be happy without him, and I loved him dearly."

Though they were severely tested, the husband and wife survived the ordeal with their faith intact. During their nearly seventy-year marriage, they served in many capacities. The husband was called to the Quorum of the Twelve at age sixty-six, and over the next thirty years his gentle manner, humor, and enthusiasm endeared him to Saints throughout the world.

LeGrand and Ina Jane Ashton Richards were in their forties when their son LeGrand A. Richards died. Thirteen family members, including their parents, made the sad trip from Utah for LeGrand A.'s funeral. Church President Heber J. Grant, who happened to be in California at the time, delayed his return to Salt Lake City so he could console the family and speak at the funeral.

LeGrand Sr. wrote of his son: "At the time of his death, LeGrand stood six feet tall and weighed 150 pounds. He was a teacher in the Aaronic Priesthood. The principal of his high school in Glendale [California] came to the house and told Ina that LeGrand was the finest boy he had ever had in his school. I used to take him with me on my visits to the various wards of the stake, and returning home, he would say, 'My Daddy, I don't see how anyone could listen to you and not believe the gospel is true.'"

Later, after performing the temple work for his grandson LeGrand A., apostle George F. Richards wrote to LeGrand: "I was ordained and endowed for LeGrand last evening in the Temple. President Grant and President Clawson were in the company of 164. . . . I am sure LeGrand was ready to receive these saving ordinances, and I am happy to have had the privilege of representing him in that sacred work."

Ina was indeed a long time healing from LeGrand A.'s death. "Life and sickness are so uncertain," she wrote. "I seem to have lost most of my courage. Maybe with study and prayer I can rebuild; we have much to be courageous about." Part of her healing came eight months after losing her son when she was in Utah for the births of her and LeGrand's first two grandchildren, Barbara Ruth Boyer and Carla Ann Iverson.

A Deadly
Tornado

In the spring of 1860, a woman who played a key role in the early
history of the Church traveled with her son to Amboy, Illinois
(about seventy miles west of Chicago), to attend a conference and visit
relatives. Several of her brothers and sisters lived in the area, as well
as her aunt, uncle, and cousin. She would have been particularly
pleased to see her younger sister and brother-in-law, Tryal and Michael
Morse, whom she had not seen for almost thirty years.

Michael had at one time been a Methodist minister. He and Tryal,
now in their fifties, had witnessed historic moments of the restoration
of the gospel. A year earlier they had moved from New York and purchased a farm on the outskirts of Amboy, a bustling community of
almost 2,000 people, where Charles Dickens's brother worked as a
newspaper editor. When Tryal's sister arrived, the couple may well
have surprised her by introducing their twenty-nine-year-old daughter, whom they had named after her.

Only two months after this reunion, on the evening of Sunday,
3 June 1860, a series of tornadoes swept across Iowa and northern
Illinois. The Morse family may have had little warning or no warning
at all as the dark twister descended on their farm. They watched help-
lessly as trees crashed to the ground and fences vanished. Then the
outbuildings collapsed, and the house virtually exploded. Tryal disappeared as she was swept up into the mass of whirling debris. An hour
later, rescuers discovered her one hundred feet away, still alive. Terribly
injured, she died within minutes. Her daughter suffered two broken
legs and died nine days later.

Tryal and Emma Morse, the sister and niece of Emma Hale Smith, were the only persons killed in the Amboy area by the unpredictable tornado. Thirty years earlier, Michael and Tryal had been living in Harmony, Pennsylvania, when Joseph and Oliver Cowdery were translating the Book of Mormon. Michael later reported that on more than one occasion he had witnessed Joseph using the seer stone to translate. His account of the translation process—which is consistent with those of David Whitmer, Elizabeth Cowdery, and several others—fully supports Emma's statement that Joseph did not use books or manuscripts to produce the Book of Mormon.

Emma was fifty-six and her son Joseph III twenty-seven when they made the trip from Nauvoo to Amboy to visit relatives and attend a conference of the Reorganized Church. The loss of her sister and niece was one in a lifelong series of hardships that Emma endured. Three years earlier, her mother-in-law and friend of three decades, Lucy Mack Smith, had died in Emma's home at age eighty-one. (Lucy had lived with Emma and her second husband, Lewis Bidamon, for the last five years of her life.)

Just weeks after the catastrophe in Amboy, Emma experienced a joyous event when two nephews from Utah stopped for a visit—Joseph F. Smith (Hyrum's youngest son) and Samuel H. B. Smith (Samuel's only son). They were on their way to serve missions in England. Emma's son Frederick brought them into a room in the Mansion House where she was working and asked if she knew them. They had grown from boys into men in the fourteen years since she had seen them. "She seemed to have forgotten Samuel," Joseph F. wrote to his wife Levira, "but *me* she said she would have known anywhere because I looked so much like father!!"

THE DUNGEON CALLED LIBERTY JAIL

Aboy by the name of John was the son of a leader in the early history of the Church. John's father assisted Joseph Smith as a scribe and also helped the Saints gather to Kirtland, Ohio. At the dedication of the Kirtland Temple in March of 1836, he spoke and held the audience spellbound for two and a half hours. His text was Matthew 8:18-20: " . . . And Jesus saith unto him, The foxes have holes, and the birds of the air have nests; but the Son of man hath not where to lay his head."

A person recording the event said the speaker's "whole soul appeared to be fired with his subject." The observer added, "We can truly say no one unacquainted with the manner of delivery and style of our speaker can, from reading, [form] any adequate idea of the powerful effect he is capable of producing in the minds of his hearers: And to say on this occasion he showed himself master of his subject and did well, would be doing him injustice; to say he acquitted himself with honor or did very well, would be detracting from his real merit; and to say that he did *exceeding* well; would be only halting praise."

In January of 1838, less than two years after the dedication of the temple, John's father, along with Joseph Smith and others, fled Kirtland for Missouri because of persecution. In Missouri, however, persecution only intensified, culminating in the autumn of 1838 with Governor Boggs's extermination order, the massacre at Haun's Mill—in which fifteen Saints were killed and a similar number wounded—and the Saints' surrender at Far West. As 10,000 Saints were driven from Missouri in the dead of winter, this brother, Joseph, Hyrum, and three others were imprisoned in Liberty Jail.

Liberty Jail was about fourteen feet square, with one upper room and one lower. The upper room had one small window and the lower two narrow grates. Subjected to abuse by the guards, filthy conditions, a constant nauseating odor, bitter cold, and food that was sometimes poisoned, the brethren were imprisoned in this dungeon throughout the winter. In the midst of this suffering, Joseph Smith received three of the most profound revelations in the history of the Church: sections 121, 122, and 123 of the Doctrine and Covenants.

Along with Emma Smith and Joseph Smith III, John and his mother were able to visit the prisoners. "We started rather late in the morning," he wrote, "and did not get to the jail till after dark, and they would not let us go in till the next morning. After taking breakfast at the hotel, we were taken to the jail and there remained for three days. . . ." Apparently feeling sorry for the prisoners, the jailer allowed them into the slightly more tolerable upper room for the visit.

John added: "One night [in February of 1839] a friend of Father's came riding to the back door of the jail with a horse all saddled. The man having charge of the jail, being friendly, helped him get away. [Father] bade his fellow prisoners goodbye, got on the horse, and with his guide got safely to Quincy, Illinois. His family, knowing he had left the jail, went to Quincy and joined him."

Like many other prominent Church members during this period, this brother eventually fell into disharmony and was excommunicated. He spent the last thirty years of his life out of the Church.

John became an attorney, and he and his brother visited Salt Lake City in 1863. "Brigham Young sent for us," he wrote. "He seemed glad to see us. He wanted to know if my father and mother [then in New York] would come to Salt Lake if he would send for them. He said he would send a mule train after them in the spring and he would bring them across the plains in a carriage in comfort and take care of them during life. I told them I did not think they would come. I wrote to my father and told him of President Young's offer, and in about 35 days an answer came declining the offer."

Despite this hospitality from Brigham Young, John was disillusioned by his experience with the Utah Saints. "Soon after I got home," he recorded, "I told [my father] the state of affairs in Salt Lake and, as it was all a humbug, I wanted to know how the Book of Mormon came into existence, for he owed it to his family to tell all he knew about it and should not go down to his grave with any such grave secrets.

"He said, 'My son, I will swear before God that what I have told you about the Book of Mormon is true. I did not write or have anything to do with its production, and if Joseph Smith ever got [the Book of Mormon], other [than] from that which he always told me (that an angel appeared and told him where to go to find the plates upon which the book was engraved in a hill near Palmyra), Smith guarded his secret well, for he never let me know by word or action that he got them differently, and I believe he did find them as he said, and that Joe Smith was a prophet, and this world will find it out some day.'

"I was surprised, [for he was] smarting under what he thought was the ingratitude of the Church for turning him down and not having been with them for over 25 years. I must believe he thought he was telling the truth. He was at this time in full possession of his faculties. What object had he in concealing the fact any longer if he did write it? My father died in 1876 at the age of 83, a firm believer in the Mormon Church."

Studious and religious from a young age, Sidney Rigdon became a popular Baptist preacher in his home state of Pennsylvania. He later moved to Ohio and joined Alexander Campbell's religious movement. In the fall of 1830, Sidney's life was forever changed when Oliver Cowdery and Parley P. Pratt (a former member of Sidney's congregation) arrived at Sidney's home carrying a carpetbag of copies of the Book of Mormon.

As recorded in the *Times and Seasons*, "This being the first time [Sidney] had ever heard of or seen the Book of Mormon, he felt very much prejudiced at the assertion; and he replied that, 'he had one Bible which he believed was a revelation from God, and with which he pretended to have some acquaintance; but with respect to the book they had presented him, he must say that he had considerable doubt.' Upon which they expressed a desire to investigate the subject, and argue the matter; but he replied, 'No, young gentlemen, you must not argue with me on the subject; but I will read your book, and see what claim it has upon my faith, and will endeavor to ascertain whether it be a revelation from God or not.' After some farther conversation on the subject, they expressed a desire to lay the subject before the people, and requested the privilege of preaching in elder Rigdon's church, to which he readily consented. The appointment was accordingly published, and a large and respectable congregation assembled. Oliver Cowdery and Parley P. Pratt severally addressed the meeting. At the conclusion, elder Rigdon arose and stated to the congregation that the information they had that evening received, was of an extraordinary character, and certainly demanded their most serious consideration: and as the apostle advised his brethren 'to prove all things, and hold fast to that which is good,' so he would exhort his brethren to do likewise, and give the matter a careful investigation; and not turn against it, without being fully convinced of its being an imposition, lest they should, possibly, resist the truth."

This kind of open-mindedness allowed Sidney to recognize the truth of the Book of Mormon. Oliver and Parley stayed with him that night and left a copy of the Book of Mormon with him the next morning before departing for Kirtland. His son John Wickliffe Rigdon wrote that his father immediately began reading the Book of Mormon, becoming so engrossed that it was hard for him to stop for meals. He read night and day and pondered deeply over what he had read.

"At length Pratt and his two companions got back," John wrote. "My father asked them who this Joseph Smith was and how much education he had. They said he was a man about 22 years old and had hardly a common school education. My father replied if that was all the education he had, he never wrote the book. Pratt told my father that they . . . would be pleased to have him and his wife come down and see them [in Kirtland]. . . . My father promised that they would and did so, and while there and before they left for Mentor, they were both baptized. . . ."

Although critics have frequently claimed Sidney Rigdon was somehow involved in writing the Book of Mormon, this account, as well as Sidney's statements at the end of his life, offer compelling evidence that he was not.

Sidney's testimony had a powerful effect on his son John, who joined the Church in 1904. In discussing his father, John added this postscript:

"After my father's death, I told Mother what my father had told me about the Book of Mormon. She said, 'Your father told you the truth. He did not write it, and I know, as he could not have written it without my knowing it, for we were married several years before the book was published, and if he wrote it, it must have been since our marriage. I was present and so was your sister Athalia Rigdon, who was a girl of about ten years old when the book was presented to your father, and she remembers the circumstances as well as any recollections of her life.'"

ESCAPING THE
MEXICAN REVOLUTION

Early in the twentieth century, two sisters grew up in the peaceful village of Colonia Juarez, Mexico, which was founded as a Mormon colony in 1885. The younger girl was born deaf, and her older sister later wrote: "Mary, my sister [four years] younger than I, was my special care, and since she was deaf, it was sometimes a real responsibility. Mother insisted that I should take her to parties with me. This was a trial, for many times I felt she hadn't been invited."

The older sister was a popular student who got good grades. At the time she started high school, the community, which included a co-op, a harness shop and tannery, and a gristmill, had a thriving economy. She recalled that homes were "well stocked with provisions: preserved fruits and vegetables in pantries, barreled pork, beans, flour, cornmeal . . . and squash in cellars. . . . Colonia Juarez had no saloons, no pool halls, no problem with drunkenness."

But this tranquil world was turned upside down when rebel leaders such as Emiliano Zapata and Pancho Villa refused to submit to Mexican presidential authority. The older sister recalled: "In the colonies by 1911 the rebels demanded horses, saddles, and food from the colonists, paying with worthless receipts, and they stole anything they could get their hands on. Father lost dozens of head of cattle and horses. We lived in dread."

Church leaders decided to send the women and children to El Paso, Texas, for safety. Thinking they would soon return, the sisters— like their friends—hid valuables in unlikely places. Then they boarded a train. "The trip to the border at El Paso was only about 150 miles, but the train went at a snail's pace and stopped every few miles. We were in terror all the time lest the rebels waylay us. We traveled all day and all night."

The family was never able to return to Mexico and lost virtually everything. Mary attended a school for the deaf and then returned home to live with her parents. The older sister married when she was twenty-two. She and her husband had four children; he established a successful business, was elected district governor of the Rotary Club, and served as a stake president. Not long after the couple's twenty-fifth wedding anniversary, the husband was called to the Quorum of the Twelve. Meanwhile, Mary, unmarried, continued to live at home.

When the sisters' mother died of stomach cancer in 1954, Mary came to live with her older sister's family, where she spent the last twenty-five years of her life. In her early eighties she survived an operation for cancer and returned to live with the family. A few months after that, however, Mary died quietly in her sleep. The night she died, Mary happened to be staying overnight with another sister, Caroline.

The older sister recalled: "I nearly had hysterics when Caroline called me. Rationally I am grateful Mary passed away so peacefully, but emotionally I felt that after all these years I had abandoned her at the last, that I should have been with her when she died, that my home was her home. She had been my special charge ever since we were children, and I felt very close to her.

"We made arrangements for her funeral in the ward for the deaf, where she had so many friends. A large crowd of relatives and friends . . . gathered to pay Mary honor. Some of the participants used sign language and others spoke aloud; each was translated for the other group. I was well satisfied with the service. . . . Mary would be pleased."

Mary Eyring and Camilla Eyring Kimball were the daughters of Edward Christian Eyring and Caroline Cottam Romney Eyring. Their younger brother, Henry Eyring, grew up to be a world-renowned scientist. After fleeing Mexico, the family lived for a time in a refugee camp in El Paso, Texas. Speaking of her father, Camilla wrote: "It is hard to imagine the disappointment he felt in losing his ranch, cattle, horses, and homes, all left to despoilers, but he turned to the task at hand, or reestablishing himself and providing for his family."

At age seventeen, Camilla moved to Provo, Utah, to live with relatives while she attended BYU. She later taught school at the Millard Academy in Hinckley, Utah, and at the Gila Academy in Thatcher, Arizona. She met Spencer W. Kimball at a bus stop in Thatcher, Arizona, and they were married on 16 November 1917, when they were both twenty-two.

In 1937, Spencer's Rotary district voted to reward his excellent club service by paying his travel expenses to the International Convention in Nice, France. While Spencer and Camilla traveled to France, Italy, and Canada, Mary stayed with their children Andrew, Olive Beth, and Edward. (Their oldest son, LeVan, was then serving in the Canadian Mission.) "Mary takes mighty good care of them," Camilla wrote.

In 1968, when Spencer received a speaking assignment at the Juarez Stake Conference, Camilla and Mary were able to return to their childhood home for the first time since they left in haste in 1912. "As soon as we were settled," wrote Camilla, "we set out on a walking tour of the little town. The little house where Mary and I were born is still standing, a small red brick home with a porch across the front. Memories came rushing back. What fun it was to relive my childhood experiences!"

"I Was Called to the Bedside of My Wife"

Ethel was called to the Relief Society General Board in 1918, when she was twenty-nine. Although she was running a household that eventually included twelve children, she was a talented woman and devoted herself to the calling, especially the talks she gave while visiting stakes. Her children recalled that she would study late at night, writing and rewriting her talks. Amy Brown Lyman, president of the Relief Society General Board, and later general president of the Relief Society, noted that Ethel "was one of the most brilliant women I ever knew. I considered her the finest writer and speaker I had on my board."

Ethel and her husband had a close relationship. Writing of her husband, she said, "[He] is most gentle, and if he feels that he has been unjust to anyone the distance is never too far for him to go and, with loving words or kind deeds, erase the hurt. He welcomes gladly the young people to his home and is never happier than when discussing with them topics of the day—sports or whatever interests them most. He enjoys a good story and is quick to see the humor of a situation."

After eighteen years on the general board, Ethel had to be released because of poor health. She suffered from a nervous condition that sometimes plunged her into depression and other times left her unable to rest. Despite the love of her husband and children, priesthood blessings, and hospitalizations, she continued to decline. On 26 August 1937, her husband wrote in his journal: "I was called to the bedside of my wife who was suddenly stricken. . . . [She] continued to grow worse until all nerve centers ceased, resulting in her death this afternoon."

Ethel Reynolds Smith was only forty-seven when she died of a cerebral hemorrhage. "She has been ailing for many months," wrote her husband, Joseph Fielding Smith, "and in spite of all aid passed away at 3:15 today. A better woman could not be found, or truer wife and mother." The daughter of George Reynolds, of the First Council of the Seventy, and Amelia Jane Schofield, Ethel had married Joseph in 1908, after his first wife, Louie Shurtliff, died at age thirty-one. Louie left two daughters, Josephine and Julina, whom Ethel raised along with her own nine children. (Another child was added to the family when they took in their newspaper carrier, Stanley Dixon, who was orphaned when he was twelve years old.)

Among the speakers at Ethel's funeral was Joseph's longtime friend David O. McKay, then serving as second counselor to President Heber J. Grant. Elder McKay had also spoken at Louie's funeral, almost thirty years earlier. Born within three years of each other (David in 1873 and Joseph in 1876), the two men shared the distinction of serving together as apostles for fifty-nine years, longer than any other two individuals.

In June of 1966, when David O. McKay was Church president and Joseph Fielding Smith was serving as one of his counselors, the two friends made one last trip together. Despite traveling throughout the world on Church assignments, President McKay, ninety-three, had never been to key Church historic sites in Missouri, and he asked Joseph, who was then ninety, to accompany him. Together they visited Liberty Jail, Far West, and Adam-ondi-Ahman. Not long after that, President McKay's health made it impossible for him to travel or speak at conference. When he died in January of 1970, Joseph Fielding Smith became the tenth president of the Church.

KILLED ON A
MISSION TO THE INDIANS

When a young woman joined the Church in West Virginia at age fifteen, she had no way of knowing the prominent role she would play in Church history over the next seventy years. Within a few years, she moved to Nauvoo and married the man who had brought her family the gospel. She later wrote: "I love my husband dearly. I believe but few in this wide world have been as happy as we have been. We have no differences, always agree on all points; our religion and our future hopes and expectations are the same."

A special blessing came on 17 March 1842, when this woman was one of the original twenty members at the founding of the Relief Society in a room above Joseph Smith's red brick store. At one Relief Society meeting, this sister heard Joseph Smith warn of his own death:

"He opened the meeting by prayer," she later wrote. "His voice trembled very much, after which he addressed us. He said: 'According to my prayer I will not be with you long to teach and instruct you, and the world will not be troubled with me much longer.'"

Four months after the first Relief Society meeting, this woman gave birth to a son; the couple named him George. Not long after that, they were blessed to receive the temple ordinances directly from the Prophet Joseph Smith. The wife later remembered, " . . . [Joseph Smith] said that we did not know how to pray to have our prayers answered. But when I and my husband had our endowments . . . Joseph Smith presiding, he taught us the order of prayer."

With the fulfillment of Joseph's prophecy, this family was driven with other Saints across the frozen Mississippi River. The wife eloquently recorded, "I will not try to describe how we traveled through storms of snow[,] wind and rain, how roads had to be made, bridges built, and rafts constructed; how our poor animals had to drag on day after day with scanty food; how our camps suffered from poverty, sickness and death. We were consoled in the midst of these hardships by having our public and private meetings in peace, praying and singing the songs of Zion, and rejoicing that we were leaving our persecutors far behind. . . . The Lord was with us, and his power was made manifest daily in our journey."

At Winter Quarters, on 11 March 1847, the woman suffered the death of her mother. Three weeks later, after a very difficult labor that lasted three days, the woman gave birth to a son named John, who lived for only four hours. The ordeal left her in poor health for several months and unable to bear any more children.

Showing a strength unusual even among stalwart pioneers, the wife chose to remain in Winter Quarters to care for her husband's family while he went west with the first company of Saints. When she finally made the trek to Utah in 1849, she made a genuine home from a Conestoga wagon:

"On this journey my wagon was provided with projections, of about eight inches wide, on each side of the top of the box. The cover, which was high enough for us to stand erect, was widened by these projections. A frame was laid across the back part of our wagon, and was corded as a bedstead; this made our sleeping very comfortable. Under our beds we stowed our heaviest articles. We had a door in one side of the wagon cover, and on the opposite side a window. A step-ladder was used to ascend to our door, which was between the wheels. . . . I had, hanging up on the inside a looking-glass, candlestick, pin-cushion, etc. In the center of our wagon we had room for four chairs, in which we and our two children sat and rode when we chose. The floor of our traveling house was carpeted, and we made ourselves as comfortable as we could under the circumstances."

After enduring so much, the family faced another tragedy several years later. In her autobiography, the woman wrote of her son George's violent, premature death: "[He] was appointed and set apart to go with Brother Jacob Hamblin on a mission to the Moquis Indians, as he was apt in learning the Indian language, and could talk the Ute dialect; it was designed that he should learn the Moquis language. He left home on the 4th of September 1860 [at age eighteen] and had traveled about seven hundred miles, when on the 2d of November he was killed by Navajo Indians, the others of the party had to return or they would have been killed also. Up to this time it was supposed the Navajos were in perfect peace with the whites, but a detachment of the United States army had a short time before attacked a Navajo village and had murdered about two hundred and fifty old men, squaws, and children, and had destroyed forty thousand head of sheep. The men of the village were on a hunt in the vicinity of the Colorado at the time of the attack about two hundred miles from their village. After they heard of the destruction of their families and property our son . . . was the first white man they saw, hence their terrible act. The traveling companions of our dear son had to leave his body in order to save their own lives. Brother Hamblin and party came home, he took about twenty men and went back again, to try to recover the body of our poor boy. They only succeeded in finding three bones and a lock of hair. We buried them in a stone vault beside his Grandfather and Grandmother in our orchards and erected a stone slab there bearing an appropriate inscription."

Bathsheba Wilson Smith, fourth general president of the Relief Society, was a loyal and devoted woman. As a girl, she had a close friend whose last name was Wilson. The two girls traded names as a symbol of friendship, and Bathsheba used Wilson as her middle name for the rest of her life, though her maiden name was Bigler. After her baptism, she showed similar devotion to the cause of the gospel, enduring trials with an uncommon grace and perseverance.

After she and her husband, George A. Smith, crossed the plains, the family lived for a time in wagons. Then George began constructing a house for Bathsheba, but before he finished he was called on a colonizing mission to Parowan, 250 miles south of Salt Lake City. He departed, leaving Bathsheba and her son and daughter in the Salt Lake Valley. Making his journey over the hot, unfriendly terrain of southern Utah, George discovered a package that Bathsheba had hidden in the wagon—a sugar loaf with English currants and a poem reading in part,

> Now I give it unto thee,
> That comfort you may in this,
> My great large sugar kiss.

George A. Smith, a cousin and friend of Joseph Smith and grandfather to Church president George Albert Smith, was sustained as first counselor to Brigham Young in 1868. Seven years later, at the age of fifty-eight, he died from complications of a punctured lung he had suffered years earlier on one of his many missions.

"His head lay . . . against my bosom," Bathsheba wrote. "Good angels had come to receive his precious spirit, perhaps our sons, prophets, patriarchs . . . but he was gone my light, my sun, my life, my joy, my Lord, yea almost my God. . . . I must not mourn but prepare myself to meet him but O my heart sinks within my bosom nearly."

Living the last thirty-five years of her life as a widow, Bathsheba was, in the words of Emmeline B. Wells, "always stately and somewhat majestic, a woman one would be sure to notice more than casually." She kept an immaculate house and raised roses, lilacs, larkspur, and hollyhocks in her garden. A counselor in the general Relief Society presidency from 1888 to 1901, she also served tirelessly in both the Endowment House and the Salt Lake Temple.

"It is a lovely and an inspiring sight to see this high priestess of righteousness arrayed in her simple white gown of home-made silk," Susa Young Gates wrote, "her dark eyes still bright, her fair, delicate face crowned with lustrous bands of shining white hair, her finely shaped head, with its rich, white lace draping, held erect, as her stately figure moves down the long aisle. The sweet smile of welcome greets all alike in its impartial graciousness. She is indeed the Elect Lady, and wisdom and peace crown her days."

Called as general Relief Society president in 1901, Bathsheba emphasized self-sufficiency for women and introduced classes in such subjects as marriage, prenatal care, parenting, and reverence. She served until she died on 20 September 1910, the last surviving member of the original Relief Society. Her remarkable influence then continued when the next president, Emmeline B. Wells, chose as her counselors Bathsheba's stepdaughter Clarissa Smith Williams (who would later become a general Relief Society president) and Bathsheba's niece Julina Lambson Smith, mother to Joseph Fielding Smith, who had lived with Bathsheba for several years.

"EVERYTHING
REMINDED ME OF HER"

W hen she was in her sixties, the wife of an apostle began experiencing major health problems, including severe headaches, periodic memory loss, and disorientation. Despite treatment and tests over a period of years, neurologists were unable to pinpoint the cause of her illness. When a surgeon recommended a shunt operation, the apostle confided in his journal: "I felt the need to go to the temple where I could be alone, and after returning, I called [my children]. Each of them expressed the opinion that if this is the only thing that might give relief, the risk should be assumed."

The operation was only partially effective, and when his wife began to develop adult-onset diabetes, the apostle arranged for a woman to stay with his wife and care for her during the day. He continued with his heavy responsibilities as a member of the Quorum of the Twelve and took care of his wife at night, going for long periods of time on little sleep. Whenever his calling took him away from Salt Lake City, he called regularly to check on his wife, but her health continued to decline.

Ten years after her symptoms first appeared, the wife suffered a cerebral hemorrhage, with doctors predicting she would never walk again. Her husband took care of her and took her regularly to her favorite hairdresser, though she was no longer able to communicate. "Although the doctors have said she would not be able to walk," he wrote hopefully, "she is now able to stand if she is supported, and this morning by [my] holding her hands and leading her, she was able to walk from the bedroom to the kitchen."

When another stroke brought additional health problems and left his wife unable to recognize her surroundings, the husband finally agreed to have her admitted to a rest home. He chose a center five miles from his home and then began visiting his wife daily or even twice a day. "Each day I have the hope that she will be better, but the progress is slow," he wrote. "Most of the time her eyes are closed, and she doesn't seem to recognize me."

The visits continued day after day, month after month, with the husband always making his wife comfortable and talking to her about the family's love for her. Then, a year and a half after the initial cerebral hemorrhage, on a day when the apostle returned to Salt Lake City on a late-afternoon flight, he was met at the airport by his family doctor and close friend. "He said, '[She] has left us. She passed away just an hour ago.' I was heartsick. We walked out of the terminal together and he drove me to the Church Administration Building where I had left my car. On the way, he talked about how much better this was for her and, of course, I knew this if she could not get well, but it did not take away the pain I felt knowing that she was gone." The couple had been married for fifty-two years.

They drove to the nursing home, where a nurse told the apostle his wife had passed away peacefully, "from deep breathing to soft, quiet breathing which gradually stopped." The husband stayed with his wife until the funeral director arrived. "As I drove home," he wrote, "the full impact of what had happened commenced to make an impression on me [that] this was the last trip I would make to see her at the nursing home after going there at least once a day for the past eighteen months. When I got home the house seemed cold, and as I walked about, everything reminded me of her."

Ordained a member of the Quorum of the Twelve Apostles in 1959 at age fifty-one, Howard W. Hunter lost his wife Clara May (Claire) Jeffs Hunter on 9 October 1983. Speakers at the funeral services three days later included President Gordon B. Hinckley, then serving as second counselor to President Kimball, and Elder Thomas S. Monson and Elder James E. Faust of the Twelve. Speaking of Claire Hunter, Elder Faust said, "This queenly woman must have been one of God's great and noble women to have commanded so much love and so much cherishing—so much respect, devotion, admiration and loving care from her eternal companion. This was reciprocated by Clara even though after a time she became diminished. At times she would smile and respond only to Howard. The tenderness which was evident in their communication was heartrending and touching. I have never seen such an example of devotion of a husband to his wife. It has been a many-splendored love affair."

During the time he was caring for his wife, Howard had several health problems of his own, including mumps, the removal of a tumor, and a heart attack. In the mid-1980s, he faced even more serious difficulties. After surviving heart-bypass surgery and bleeding ulcers, he began experiencing excruciating pain due to deteriorating bones in his lower back. The condition also triggered serious pain in the legs, often for extended periods of time. Howard was eventually confined to a wheelchair, with doctors predicting he would not be able to stand or walk again.

Despite this prognosis, Howard combined exercise, therapy, and prayer in a long, patient effort to walk again. Almost a year and a half after he began using a wheelchair, he wrote:

"There was a last and a first today. The temple meeting was the last for the year 1988, and it was the first temple meeting since August 13,

1987, that I have not been in a wheelchair. Today I went to the temple on a walker. It was slow and laborious, but I was able to do it with Neil [Neil McKinstry, a Church security guard] walking by my side to catch me if I would fall. When I came into the council room, the brethren stood and clapped. This is the first time I have heard clapping in the temple. They have been extremely kind and solicitous of me, and in nearly every prayer that has been offered in the last year or so, I have been prayed for. Most of the doctors have told me that I would never be able to stand or walk, but they have failed to take into consideration the power of prayer."

In April of 1990, while he was serving as president of the Quorum of the Twelve, and almost seven years after Claire had died, Howard made an announcement at a regular Thursday morning meeting of the Twelve. "Inis Stanton is an old acquaintance from California. I've been visiting with her for some time, and I've decided to be married."

President Hunter's family, as well as his fellow apostles, were thrilled with this news. They were also surprised when Howard informed them the temple ceremony would be small and private. The only people present were Howard, Inis, President Hinckley, who performed the sealing, President Monson, and Inis's bishop.

Although his health problems intensified, President Hunter served actively as president of the Twelve until President Ezra Taft Benson died in 1994, at which time President Hunter became the fourteenth president of the Church. In his first public statement as president, he made an oft-quoted request of Church members: "I would invite all members of the Church to live with ever more attention to the life and example of the Lord Jesus Christ, especially the love and hope and compassion He displayed. I pray that we might treat each other with more kindness, more courtesy, more humility and patience and forgiveness."

"Friends at First Are Friends Again at Last": The Fellowship of the Saints

"A Fully Satisfactory Golf Shot"

An apostle, who at times in his life had suffered ill health as a result of stress, worried about his friend, a fellow apostle six years his junior, who was a virtual workaholic. The younger apostle had taken up golf years earlier and found it a wonderful way to relax and have an enjoyable time with friends. Over a period of time he tried to convince his friend, who of course had never golfed, of the therapeutic value of the game.

The younger apostle persisted and finally convinced his friend to try golfing and stick with it until he hit a drive that rated as "a real golf shot." Accordingly, the two men proceeded on an agreed date to Nibley Park, where they were joined by several other golfers. When it was finally the friend's turn to try, he shocked the gallery of observers by stepping up to the ball, swinging confidently, and hitting a 200-yard drive that stayed in the fairway. The crowd burst into applause.

"Congratulations," said the younger apostle. "That was a fine shot."

"You mean *that* was a fully satisfactory golf shot?" asked the novice.

"It certainly was," came the reply.

"Then I have fulfilled my part of the agreement?"

"You have—and don't you feel the thrill of excitement? Now you'll be playing regularly."

"Thank you," said the friend. "But if I have carried out my part of the agreement, then I shall call on you to live up to yours. You promised that if I hit a satisfactory drive and did not feel the spontaneous desire to play, you would stop urging me to do so. Now I should like to get back to the office, where I have a great deal of work waiting." With that irony, the friend walked briskly off the course and never returned.

President Heber J. Grant and Apostle James E. Talmage remained great friends despite President Grant's inability to convince Elder Talmage of the pleasures of golf. James Talmage was a studious man who took his work seriously; yet despite his dedication to weightier matters he had a humorous side, as seen in the golfing incident.

James's son John recounted another anecdote that reveals the more personal side of the scientist and theologian. It happened while James was serving as president of the University of Utah in the 1890s. One night he arrived home bruised and bleeding, with clothes torn and muddy. His wife, May, feared he had been the victim of violence, but he explained that was not the case. Riding his bicycle home from the office, he had attempted to cross a single-plank footbridge without dismounting the bike. "For the next hour, the president of the University of Utah might have been observed trundling his bicycle fifty yards or so down the road from the bridge, mounting and riding furiously toward the plank crossing, turning onto it with grim-lipped determination—and plunging off it in a spectacular and bone-shaking crash into the rough ditchbank." The spunky professor finally proceeded home after crossing several times in a row without mishap.

INSTRUCTIONS FOR HIS OWN FUNERAL

Years before his death, a beloved Church leader left specific instructions for his own funeral: "I feel . . . patriotism for my church and my people [and] . . . would die—willingly if necessary—but if this fight is ever over, I do not hanker for any more battles. Believing I am a soldier, I ask . . . to be buried like a soldier.

1. My fellow comrades are to preside and arrange the services.

2. Martial music.

3. Violin solos of the inspiring kind, with quartettes and songs that are befitting the occasion.

4. Short prayers.

5. Brief addresses, remembering always that these services are for me and no one else.

6. No person to speak who did not love and understand the deceased.

7. The subjects uppermost in the minds of the speakers must be:

a. What was his character and what was his general influence, taken as a whole, through the course of years among his people?

b. Did he have any special attraction for the narrow and intolerant?

c. Was he tolerant, charitable, intelligent, unselfish, and self-sacrificing?

d. Was the Golden Rule his great morality and his practical guide?

e. Did he believe that justice means a free and equal chance of life's happiness to all, and that there can be no rest this side of justice?"

Answering his own questions, the incomparable J. Golden Kimball said:

"Yes, I believe in all this and have endeavored to train myself along these broad and generous lines. My failure in not reaching my goal has been due to my weakness and not to the fact that I did not believe it.

"I believe this great goal is to be won through the grace of God and by the influence of His Holy Spirit, by the morality of toleration, freedom of thought, brotherly love, and charity to all men—not the charity of alms-giving, but that charity which is forgiveness and love.

"My closing testimony is that I have unfaltering faith in God the Father, and in His Son, Jesus Christ, my Redeemer, and in the Holy Ghost."

Though thirty years Elder Kimball's junior, Hugh B. Brown became a good friend. The two had much in common—a sharp sense of humor, a certain unwillingness to conform to convention, and training in the school of hard knocks.

J. Golden's mother, Christeen Kimball, widow of apostle Heber C. Kimball, moved the family from Salt Lake City to Bear Lake, Idaho, when J. Golden was a teenager. He remembered: "There was no house or improvement, and we commenced a fight for life. God knows it was a hard fight with poverty and terrible blizzards in winter. . . . We worked, we toiled early and late. . . ."

Hugh had a surprisingly similar experience when his family moved from the Salt Lake Valley to Canada: "We arrived on my [sixteenth] birthday and found that the only provision for our family was a two-room log house. There were ten of us in the family at the time. We boys slept in tents that were pitched outside. The first winter was very cold and was a real trial to us city boys who had never had to experience anything like that in our lives."

When fifty-three-year-old Hugh was called to be president of the British Mission in 1937, J. Golden, then eighty-four, admonished President Brown to "give 'em h——- over there, Hugh, give 'em h——-."

A year later, Elder Kimball, who had served in the First Council of the Seventy for forty-six years, was killed in an automobile accident near Reno, Nevada. Hugh B. Brown, his friend and fellow soldier in the cause, had previously summed up J. Golden Kimball's unique appeal in a way meeting all the requirements outlined for his funeral:

"[He] dares to be himself. His life is so simple and his words so direct that we never spend time trying to look through the surface to find the man, for there is no veneer—he is solid oak.

"He is a philosopher and humorist, with a droll and scintillating way of expressing himself. He was trained in the University of Hard Knocks, and he has a vocabulary all his own. He has kept a sense of humor in the Church, and believes the 'trip to heaven' should be a joyous one. Every group is made happier by his presence, and when he leaves us the angels will greet him with a smile.

"He is one of the few remaining examples of the rugged West, as honest as a cactus, as tender as a rose. Through a long life of actual contact with, and deep understanding of his fellow-man, he has achieved the educated heart, which is always set in the direction of true kindness; it functions without deliberate thought.

"The young people of the Church love him because he is so human, so natural, so devoid of pretense.

"No man will ever fill the unique position held by J. Golden Kimball in the hearts of the people."

A Church President,
a U.S. President, and
an Entrepreneur

※——☓——※

Born within five years of each other, and in the same state, two men whose names would both become famous learned to work hard as boys. The younger of the two later said, "I am grateful . . . to my father for giving me an opportunity to develop my individuality and my sense of responsibility. . . . He would send me out to the sheep camp on an assignment but would tell me little about what I was to do or where I was to find the sheep. Even when I was a little boy, such problems were for me to solve, for my father never did my thinking for me."

The older boy was also initiated into the world of work by tending livestock—in his case, cows. At nine years old he regularly milked from two to nine cows, memorizing the Articles of Faith, the Ten Commandments, and a variety of hymns as he worked. Years later, after being called as an apostle, he said, "Brothers and Sisters: I don't know exactly why the Lord has called me, but I do have one talent to offer. My father taught me how to work; and if the Lord can use a worker, I'm available."

Both of these men moved from their native state and became successful businessmen elsewhere. Both became admired for their ability to work hard. Over the years they became friends. Both served as stake presidents. The older man was called to be an apostle, and thirty years later he was ordained president of the Church. Less than a year later, the younger man wrote to him:

"I didn't have a chance to tell you, but I sure was thrilled when I heard you talk about a clean-up program for the homes and farms in the State of Utah. I was really surprised that you gave the program such quick action, but I do know that follow-through on it will give our whole state the wholesome appearance that it should have.

"You did a wonderful job of conducting the Conference and your speeches couldn't have been more appropriate. . . . May the Lord continue to bless you in all that you do. [My wife] joins in sending our love and best wishes."

The younger man, who had become a well-known entrepreneur, was instrumental in arranging a meeting between the Church president and the vice president of the United States. The entrepreneur and his wife joined the vice president and his family when they arrived in Salt Lake City. After a performance by the Tabernacle Choir, the First Presidency and the entrepreneur met privately with the vice president. Later the vice president, the president of the Church, and the entrepreneur—with their wives—joined others for a luncheon in the Church Office Building.

Within months, a national crisis occurred that brought about the vice president's swearing in as president of the United States. Not long after that, the Church president offered the opening prayer at a session of the United States Senate, and the entrepreneur and the Church president arranged for the First Lady and her daughter to tour a newly completed temple.

This three-way friendship continued two years later when the entrepreneur organized a national celebration in the nation's capital. The Church president was invited to the White House, where he met privately with the U.S. president and presented him with a statuette representing a pioneer family. On the same trip, the Church president and his wife were asked to be the guests of the U.S. president and his wife at the national celebration. They sat in the presidential box while the Tabernacle Choir and others performed. As they had on previous occasions, the U.S. president and his wife proved to be gracious hosts.

When Gerald Ford, his wife Betty, and their son John visited Salt Lake City in June of 1974, the Tabernacle Choir arranged to sing "Eternal Father, Strong to Save," a favorite of Vice President Ford, and "Lead Kindly Light" and "Battle Hymn of the Republic," favorites of Mrs. Ford. President Spencer W. Kimball and J. Willard Marriott then met with Vice President Ford while Sister Kimball and Mrs. Ford toured the Beehive House.

Two months later, at the resignation of Richard M. Nixon, Gerald Ford became the thirty-eighth president of the United States. Nixon had selected Ford as vice president when Spiro T. Agnew resigned in 1973. Gerald Ford thus became the first U.S. president who was elected neither to the presidency nor the vice presidency.

Spencer W. Kimball was born in 1895 and J. Willard Marriott in 1900, both in Utah. They settled in Arizona and Washington, D.C., respectively, and raised their families in those locations. Because President Kimball had suffered ill health prior to becoming Church president, some expected his administration to be uneventful. Quite the opposite turned out to be true. To mention just a few events that occurred during his presidency—two revelations were added to the Pearl of Great Price, the First Quorum of the Seventy was reorganized, the priesthood was made available to all worthy males, and the consolidated meeting schedule was instituted.

J. Willard Marriott's generosity made possible the Marriott Center at Brigham Young University, the Marriott Library at the University of Utah, and the J. Willard Marriott Allied Health Sciences Building at Weber State University. Throughout his career, he continually strengthened the public image of the Church through his good will and good deeds.

A Friend
to Children

Born in 1897 in Provo, Utah, Joan was a talented student and musician. By the age of fourteen she was serving as Sunday School organist in her ward. She received a dual degree from Brigham Young University in music and education and then did graduate work at the University of California at Berkeley, Columbia University, and the University of Utah. She had a special way with children and taught school in Provo and Draper, eventually being appointed supervisor of primary education in the Jordan School District of Salt Lake County.

In 1937, Joan became engaged to E. Ray Beck, a widower with three children who was serving as bishop of the Sandy Utah Third Ward. Two weeks before their planned wedding, Ray died unexpectedly. One of his children, Geniel, chose to live with Joan after her father's death. Joan raised Geniel as her own daughter.

Joan became a well-known educator and friend of youth, serving on the general boards of both the Primary and the Young Women's Mutual Improvement Association. While in Canada on a Church assignment, she became seriously ill and sought a blessing from Edward James Wood, president of the Alberta Canada Temple. In the blessing, President Wood "told her that one day she would be called to a position of such magnitude that at present she would not be able to contemplate it."

This blessing saw profound fulfillment when Joan was sixty-five years old. That year she renewed her acquaintance with a Church leader she had known through the years. He had lost his wife the previous year. Joan and the future Church president were married in June of 1963.

Curiously, Freda Joan Jensen had first met Harold B. Lee more than forty years earlier, when she was dating one of his former missionary companions. Joan later became good friends with Fern Tanner Lee, Harold's first wife. When Harold informed President David O. McKay of his plans to marry Joan Jensen, President McKay gave his enthusiastic blessing and said, "It is not good for a man to be alone." He later told his wife, Emma Riggs McKay, that "Joan is a wonderful girl." As Sister McKay noted, "When he says that it means something."

Fellow apostles Henry D. Moyle and Marion G. Romney were witnesses at the temple sealing of Harold and Joan, which was performed by President McKay. President Lee recorded that President McKay "was wonderful in his counsel to us before and after the ceremony was performed."

Speaking of Joan's unique gift with children, President Lee wrote: "She has the key that unlocks many a child's heart. She has the ability to teach the teacher this secret. Her conversation with a child is a beautiful thing to hear. Her skill and understanding are born of a lifetime of knowledge and application of child psychology. She is constantly reaching out to the child that is not understood."

Harold B. Lee was called into the First Presidency in 1970 (serving as a counselor to Joseph Fielding Smith) and became president of the Church in 1972. He and Joan traveled throughout the world meeting missionaries, members, and investigators. President Lee died suddenly at age seventy-four in 1973. Joan followed him in death eight years later, dying on 1 July 1981, one day before her eighty-fourth birthday.

A Lost Sheep
Returns to the Fold

E dson, the son of one of the original members of the Quorum of the
Twelve Apostles, was born in Iowa in 1862 and raised on a farm.
Like six other members of the original quorum, Edson's father lost his
place because of disharmony. Still, Edson recalled that his father was a
forceful "preacher of righteousness and my heart was made to burn
within me whenever I heard a discourse delivered by him." This early
influence eventually led Edson to join the Reorganized Church, and
he took charge of a branch of seventy people.

Eventually, however, Edson became disillusioned with his faith
and was asked to give up his preaching credentials, which he did. As
he described it, he then became "a wanderer in spiritual darkness,
not knowing which church I ought to join except the one designated
as the kingdom of God."

Edson married and had several children. He farmed and worked in
lumber camps and on railroads. He continued to believe in Christ and
hungered for religious truth. Edson preached "Christian union" for a
time but found it impossible to get different denominations to become
united even in spirit. He became a member of "the so-called Christian
church" but was soon dissatisfied. Edson's wife died after thirty-six
years of marriage, and with his children raised, he eventually found
himself in the state of Washington. One day he happened to meet two
LDS missionaries and accepted their invitation to hear the gospel.
After "thorough investigation," he was baptized on 15 February 1931
at the age of sixty-eight.

After his baptism, Edson Don Carlos Smith testified, "I am fully satisfied that this church is the true one that was organized of God through the prophet Joseph and in fact the Kingdom of God upon the earth." Edson was the son of William Smith, Joseph Smith's younger brother, who had been excommunicated in 1845.

After he joined the Church, Edson moved to Salt Lake City, and he and his second wife, Hannah Christine Hansen Olsen, were sealed in the Salt Lake Temple in 1932 by apostle George F. Richards. In 1938, Edson and Hannah attended a Smith family reunion, where they were warmly received by such relatives as George Albert Smith and Joseph Fielding Smith. Edson was recognized as the oldest direct relative of the Prophet Joseph Smith.

Speaking of his father, Edson wrote that William "ever spoke in endearing terms of his brother Joseph and held him to be a prophet of God to the end of his days. I have heard him give an account of Joseph's early calling and of the angel Moroni's visits to him and also the first vision." Edson added that William "was a good kind father and I loved him very much and still do but he surely made a sad mistake when he abandoned his calling as an apostle . . . and refused the leadership of Brigham Young. . . . But why ponder over this mistake of my father. I have seen to it that he has been reinstated in the true church and the true work of God and have received a witness from him from the spirit world that he is satisfied and pleased with his reinstatement. This represents the temple work I have done for him now. Let God be true regardless of the mistakes of men."

Edson Don Carlos Smith remained true to the faith and died in February of 1939 at age seventy-six.

A Friendship
Survives

In October of 1910, shortly after the death of general Relief Society
president Bathsheba Wilson Smith, the venerable Emmeline B. Wells
was called to replace her. Although she had not been a member of the
original Relief Society, as Sister Smith had been, she had lived in
Nauvoo as a young woman and personally knew Joseph and Emma
Smith. Eighty-two years old at the time of her call, Emmeline B. Wells
was the oldest person ever called to a major leadership position in the
Church (the oldest man named as an apostle was eighty-year-old George
Q. Morris, called in 1954). Over her rich but difficult life, Emmeline had
endured persecution in Nauvoo, the trek across the plains, the loss of
two daughters in young adulthood, and the deaths of two husbands.

Among those Emmeline called to serve with her were two strong-
willed, exceptionally intelligent women who had a major impact on
the course of the Church over a period of more than fifty years. The
elder had been born in 1856, the younger in 1872, both to prominent
fathers. Both had long experience with prominent women leaders.
Writing of visits to her home by Eliza R. Snow and Zina D. H. Young,
the younger woman said: "They came to our home on several occasions to bless and comfort my semi-invalid mother. On one occasion
we children were permitted in the room and were allowed to kneel in
prayer with these sisters, and later to hear their fervent appeals for
mother's recovery. They placed their hands upon her head and promised that through our united faith she would be spared to her family.
This was an impressive spiritual experience for us, and the fulfillment
of this promise, a testimony."

These two sisters grew close as they both served with Emmeline B. Wells throughout her ten-and-a-half year administration, one that in many ways marked a transition from the nineteenth to the twentieth century. Along with supporting women's suffrage, they also supported a more standardized outline for Relief Society lessons throughout the Church. This was something largely left to individual stakes in the past and was a movement resisted by Emmeline B. Wells herself, who expressed the "fear that in these outlines we are getting too far away from the spiritual side of our great work." In their attitude toward social work in the Church, however, these two independent women saw things quite differently.

The younger woman had received training in social work several years before her call to the Relief Society General Board, and in 1917 she was asked to attend a Red Cross convention in Denver. Not long afterwards, she returned to Denver for a six-week course at the Home Service Institute, where she and three other Relief Society delegates received training in civilian relief work. Church president Joseph F. Smith encouraged her "to devote herself to the study of family welfare work with a view of improving the LDS charity work." In addition, she began working with Salt Lake City's Charity Organization Society and was joined by Apostle George Albert Smith in this effort.

When Utah stake Relief Society leaders began integrating new social work methods with Relief Society service—such as setting up their own training institute and replacing monthly donations with an annual fund-raiser—the older woman publicly voiced her opposition. "We may need to change and modify in the Society," she wrote, "but let us not make fundamental changes nor alter the perfect and wise adjustment of our religious organization to match the world's spectacular methods lest we fall into their mistakes and partake of their errors."

The younger woman believed that professional orientation would make Relief Society sisters more effective in their service and less likely to duplicate efforts of government relief agencies. The older sister worried that institutional help might replace the more personal help of friends and neighbors, that elderly sisters would be unwilling or unable to master modern social work, and that private records (of individuals receiving financial assistance) would become public.

During the winter of 1919–20, the older woman investigated "the failures which come from administering charity through institutional and paid financial agents." She wrote to a friend on the general board, " . . . I am advised to keep quiet for a while. . . . There is strong sentiment on the other side and the popular trend is in the other direction. [The younger woman] is invited to speak in Denver next Wednesday on this subject. The title of her paper is 'Permeating an Established Relief Agency with Case Work.'"

Early in 1920, these two women and several others met with Church President Heber J. Grant to voice their varying opinions. The two sisters showed such a strong difference of opinion that they were referred back to the Relief Society general board.

Fortunately, this significant difference in viewpoints, which could have resulted in resentment and a lack of direction for the Relief Society itself, worked into a compromise. As two historians have noted, "Several things happened as a result of this full airing of differing points of view. First, the awareness that duplication of effort wasted resources and could potentially harm those in need led to a stronger working relationship between the Relief Society general presidency and the Presiding Bishopric. . . . Second, a firm commitment was made not to rely on outside agencies to administer charity to Latter-day Saints. Bishops were to be responsible for the welfare of their ward members, and Relief Society sisters were to labor under their direction. Nevertheless, charity was not to be disbursed without careful investigations as had too often been the case in the past."

More important than this institutional compromise was the personal reconciliation of Susa Young Gates and Amy Brown Lyman. Susa, the elder of the two, a daughter of Brigham Young who was often as outspoken in her views as her father, showed her considerable insight into the situation when she wrote: "My dear Sister Lyman has been just as single-hearted, as devout, and as dutiful as I could possibly be. Then, which may be right and which wrong? Perhaps both in some measure."

Despite their strong opinions, Susa and Amy each found a way to argue those opinions without making pride an issue. They were more interested in the cause of Relief Society than in winning arguments. As a result, the Relief Society organization was strengthened. Relief Society sisters serving in wards worked under the direction of their bishops, not third-party charities. At the same time, the Relief Society added a professional department (the Relief Society social services department, headed by Amy) that worked with the community at large, and many Relief Society sisters received social training that enhanced their Christlike service. The decade that followed—the turbulent 1920s—turned out to be a period of very effective service by the Relief Society.

As a young woman, Susa Young Gates had founded and edited the *Young Woman's Journal* and organized the music department at Brigham Young Academy. She published widely and served on the BYA board of directors and the Young Women's Mutual Improvement Association general board. "In times past," she wrote, "women have . . . done many improper things; and one of them is they often preferred men's opinions to their own and even yielded points of conscience for the sake of pleasing them, until, very naturally, they are looked upon by men as shallow, weak, and contemptible. . . . A course of self-reliance and self-assertion will restore our credit."

The daughter of Margaret Zimmerman Brown and Pleasant Grove, Utah, mayor and bishop John Brown, Amy Brown Lyman showed the lifelong influence of her mother. "[She] was a partial invalid for a number of years due to childbirth complications," Amy later wrote, "and during that time she directed the affairs of her household and in addition helped solve the social and economic problems of many of her friends. . . . She was a woman's woman and always maintained that girls should have equal opportunities and privileges with boys."

When Emmeline B. Wells was released as general Relief Society president in 1921, three weeks before she died at age ninety-three, Susa Young Gates turned much of her attention to genealogy and temple work. She became head of the Research Department and Library of the Genealogical Society of Utah in 1923 and compiled a catalogue of more than 16,000 names of the Young family. She died of cancer in 1933, the same year that saw the passing of B. H. Roberts and James E. Talmage.

Amy Brown Lyman continued her service as Relief Society general secretary under Clarissa Smith Williams (who succeeded Sister Wells), and in 1928 she was called as a counselor to Louise Y. Robison, the seventh general president of the Relief Society. Amy was called as president herself in 1940, and she continued to emphasize welfare work throughout her long Relief Society career.

In resolving the conflict they faced, Susa Young Gates and Amy Brown Lyman were both true to their mentor Emmeline B. Wells, who had written (in a letter to Amy) that the influence of Relief Society work "is the spirit of love and magnanimous charity that unites us in a fellowship grander and holier than the highest educational organizations among the cultured and learned women of the world."

"I Know Him Better Than Any Other Man"

When a former member of his ward was called to be an apostle, George Beard wrote a letter of approval to the First Presidency and Quorum of the Twelve. The letter offers an excellent biographical summary of the new apostle, a listing of his many admirable qualities, and an interesting look at Brother Beard himself.

"It filled my heart with joy and satisfaction to know that my friend, brother, and neighbor . . . had been selected by you as an Apostle.

"I believe I know [him] better than any other man living, and I feel that it might increase your confidence in the man you have chosen to fill that important position when I can truthfully bear testimony that he is one of the straightest, cleanest, most sincere and reliable of any man that I have ever met.

"His mother moved with her family to Coalville [Utah] and they became my next-door neighbors.

"When I acted as Bishop of the South Coalville Ward, [he] was a young man. Whenever I needed some special work done in the Ward I always selected him to do the work, as I was sure it would not be neglected and would be well done.

"I have had much business with him and have always found him to keep his word to the letter.

"I suppose one reason for my admiration and respect for him is the fact that he is a self-made man.

"He earned money to provide for his widowed mother and her family and had no opportunity to go to school.

"He secured a position as pump tender in the Wasatch Coal Mine and he surrounded himself with good books while working in that position. His selection was the New Testament, the Book of Mormon, and other Church works. (The men who attended the pumps before and after him wasted their time and their energy by smoking cigarettes.)

"He was always an eloquent, clear speaker who could make the young people understand the Gospel of Jesus Christ.

"Brother James B. Rhead . . . , [the new apostle], and myself made an agreement among ourselves that we would make mental notes when anyone of us were speaking on the stand and would try to correct each other's grammar, speech, and ideas, which we did, always with a friendly spirit.

"I believe [he] secured his education by listening to such men as B. H. Roberts, Apostle Talmage, and other members of the Church who were highly educated.

"I sincerely hope that God will bless him with health and with strength so that he can at all times do his part in assisting you Brethren in the great and grand work which you are engaged in.

"A year or so ago a photograph was printed in the *Tribune* which showed the Twelve Apostles and the Presidency of the Church.

"I took great pleasure in showing that picture to my family and . . . I believe it made an impression for good on the younger members of the family which has never left them.

"When the Apostles have the next picture taken I am sure that [he] will look just as clean and sincere as the balance of you."

Perhaps no phrase better describes Charles A. Callis than "self-made man." He was born in poverty in Ireland in 1865 and baptized ten years later, the same year he and his widowed mother sailed to America, their tickets obtained through the help of the Perpetual Emigration Fund. As Brother Beard indicated, Charles labored in the coal mines for several years, becoming well acquainted with Church works and the likes of Shakespeare in the process.

In his twenties, Charles was befriended by B. H. Roberts, of the First Council of the Seventy, who was eight years his senior. Elder Roberts had also been born in poverty in Great Britain, sailed to America as a boy, and worked hard at backbreaking jobs. Elder Roberts's influence was important in Charles's decisions to serve a mission and study law. After his mission to Great Britain, where he labored for a time in his native Ireland, Charles was elected Summit County (Utah) attorney in 1898.

Virtually all of Charles's forty-four-year marriage to Grace Pack was spent in Church service, most of it as president of the Southern States Mission, where he and Grace served from 1905 to 1933, an amazing twenty-eight years (with a break of just a few months in 1907). He was called to the Quorum of the Twelve in 1933 at age sixty-eight.

Echoing Brother Beard's sentiments, Nephi Jensen, a missionary companion of Charles A. Callis, wrote, "He is one of those heroic souls who have come up from the depths. A few years ago he was working in a coal mine . . . now he is a practicing attorney. . . . He not only acquired a knowledge of law by self effort but read widely on general subjects and trained himself in the art of public speaking. . . . He is a leader. He does things without being told. . . . While others are waiting for opportunities to do good he is making them."

Eyewitnesses to History: Encounters with Well-Known Individuals

A LETTER TO
HELEN KELLER

W hen I was superintendent of Sunday Schools," David O. McKay wrote, "we invited Helen Keller to come to Salt Lake City and speak to the children. She was blind and deaf, but not speechless, and she addressed more than seven hundred children in the Assembly Hall, and her speech was entitled 'Happiness.'

"Later, she traveled throughout the world. She was received by kings and queens and the great of the earth. She has been entertained by presidents of the United States. Many honors and degrees have been conferred upon her.

"She visited Salt Lake City several years later and spoke in the Tabernacle. As we were standing in the ante-room where the general authorities enter, prior to her appearing before the audience, the organ began to play, and, blind and deaf, but not speechless, she said, 'The organ.' She touched one of the pillars and listened to the strains of the organ through the sense of touch."

As President McKay's reminiscences indicate, Helen Keller enjoyed a long-term, friendly relationship with the Church, and Church leaders have often mentioned her as a source of inspiration.

Some may not have realized that as a devout Swedenborgian, Helen Keller had religious beliefs that sounded surprisingly familiar to Latter-day Saints. The founder of the Church, Emanuel Swedenborg (1688–1772) experienced a dramatic vision, spoke of three heavens, and even believed in a sort of eternal marriage.

Early in 1940, Helen Keller again visited Salt Lake City, where she met with President Heber J. Grant and others. She spoke in the

Tabernacle and requested Governor Herbert B. Maw to give a history of the building and its construction. During the same visit, President Grant presented Helen Keller with a seven-volume set of the Book of Mormon in Braille. Perhaps not coincidentally, Elder Levi Edgar Young quoted Swedenborg in the general conference held weeks later: "There is, however, within every soul a divine light; a divine impulse for good and truth, and when this light is developed, then life reaches its highest vision and man his greatest happiness."

Not long after that visit, Helen Keller wrote a letter to a prominent Church leader and discussed her efforts to help the blind. "As you may know," she wrote, "destiny has placed me among the co-workers with blind persons determined to hew a path out of the miseries of isolation and make good their place in society. Constantly I devise means by which help to the blind of America may be enlarged and perpetuated."

Miss Keller signed the letter in her elegant block letters. The Church leader responded:

"When one who has sight contemplates what he would miss if he did not have it, his heart strings are torn with sympathy and his soul rises to God with gratitude for the blessings which are his. I assure you I shall in the future as in the past do what is offered to me to do to help alleviate the distress and bring comfort to those who are blind. . . .

"As you may know, the Church is engaged in many activities for the relief of human suffering. The contributions which Church members give in obedience to the calls made upon them are always relatively great. As you probably know, the Church has tried and is trying to bring comfort and blessing to the blind. [This included publishing a variety of Church literature in Braille and distributing it free of charge.] This we shall continue to do.

"One is awed by the admiration one has of the great achievement which you, yourself, have made in the matter of overcoming the great tragedy of blindness. As I said to you the other day, God has greatly blessed you in other ways, and I think that you in turn might bring blessings to the blind. It is my prayerful wish that your health may continue good and that you may be able to continue your great labors for the welfare of the afflicted."

Born in 1880, Helen Keller was a year and a half old when an acute illness left her deaf and blind. With Anne Sullivan's help, she learned to read, write, and speak. She graduated with honors from Radcliffe College and then served on the Massachusetts Commission for the Blind. She traveled throughout the world to raise awareness of the needs of disabled people and to offer encouragement to those people themselves. After World War II, she visited wounded veterans in hospitals.

The Church leader, born in 1871, was a close contemporary of Helen Keller's. He also displayed brilliance as a youth and was first in his class and student body president at the University of Utah. Throughout his long service to his country and the Church, he corresponded with many nationally prominent individuals besides Helen Keller, including Herbert Hoover, Secretary of State Cordell Hull, and broadcaster Lowell Thomas.

Through his voluminous correspondence and his personal kindness, J. Reuben Clark Jr. created a great deal of goodwill for the Church. His friendship with Lowell Thomas is a typical example. Thomas was a broadcast journalist, commentator, and explorer especially noted for his association with Lawrence of Arabia. He and President Clark corresponded for several years, and President Clark frequently sent small gifts. In July of 1954, Lowell sent a letter that read in part, "Dear President Clark, My wife and I much appreciate the box of cherries that just arrived. You must have some magic soil somewhere out there in Utah. I hear they are making progress on an enlarged ski development, at Alta. . . . Look what your cherries inspired me to write! Ah well, everything that comes out of Utah seems to be full of inspiration."

Three months after he graduated from the Columbia College of Law in 1906, J. Reuben Clark Jr. was appointed to the State Department, where he served as solicitor. He left the State Department in 1913 to practice law, establishing a reputation as a top legal mind. In 1928 President Calvin Coolidge appointed him undersecretary of the State Department. Two years after that, President Herbert Hoover asked him to serve as Ambassador to Mexico. (The two men shared political views and enjoyed a lifelong friendship.)

Brother Clark was serving in Mexico in 1931 when Church President Heber J. Grant wrote and asked him to replace Charles W. Nibley as second counselor in the First Presidency. (President Nibley had died 11 December 1931.) Brother Clark's responsibilities as ambassador did not allow him to be sustained in the First Presidency until April 1933. He became first counselor at the death of Anthony W. Ivins a year and a half later and was ordained an apostle one week after that. President Clark served as counselor to Heber J. Grant, George

Albert Smith, and David O. McKay, and his period of service in the First Presidency—twenty-eight years—is longer than any other counselor. He died in 1961 at age ninety.

J. Reuben Clark Jr. and Helen Keller likely avoided the subject of politics in their conversations and correspondence. "Our real enemies," President Clark is quoted as saying, "are communism and its running mate, socialism. . . . And never forget for one moment that communism and socialism are state slavery." By contrast, Helen Keller had been a vocal socialist in the early 1900s, joining the Socialist Party of America along with such notable individuals as Jane Addams, Jack London, and Upton Sinclair. However, she seldom mentioned her political views in public after 1922 and was particularly careful not to do so in her fund-raising efforts for the blind.

The unparalleled Helen Keller continued her efforts on behalf of the blind for another quarter century, dying at the age of eighty-seven in 1968. Her powerful autobiography concludes with this passage: "Often when I dream, thoughts pass through my mind like cowled shadows, silent and remote, and disappear. Perhaps they are the ghosts of thoughts that once inhabited the mind of an ancestor. At other times the things I have learned and the things I have been taught, drop away, as the lizard sheds its skin, and I see my soul as God sees it. There are also rare and beautiful moments when I see and hear in Dreamland. What if in my waking hours a sound should ring through the silent halls of hearing? What if a ray of light should flash through the darkened chambers of my soul? What would happen, I ask many and many a time. Would the bow-and-string tension of life snap? Would the heart, overweighted with sudden joy, stop beating for very excess of happiness?"

PEARL S. BUCK'S
BOOK OF HOPE

In July of 1937, two years before Hitler invaded Poland, Japanese and Chinese forces encountered each other in a skirmish at the Marco Polo Bridge near Beijing. Japan, which had exploited a minor incident to occupy Manchuria in 1931, used the skirmish as the pretext for a full-scale invasion of China. On 13 December 1937, 50,000 troops of the Japanese Imperial Army captured China's capital city of Nanking and unleashed a reign of terror in which between 100,000 and 200,000 Chinese civilians were murdered. (Some estimates are even higher.) Other Japanese soldiers committed similar atrocities in many parts of China.

Among those who rose to China's defense was the world-famous writer Pearl S. Buck. Her parents had served as Southern Presbyterian missionaries in China, and although Pearl was born in West Virginia (while her parents were in the United States on a brief leave), she lived in China for virtually all of her first forty years. During the 1920s and early 30s, she had lived and taught in Nanking. In fighting that involved Nationalist troops, Communists, and Chinese warlords, several Westerners were killed in Nanking in 1927. Ironically, the Buck family found refuge in Japan, where they lived for one year before returning to China.

Pearl S. Buck's biographer records that although "she was tormented with ambivalence about America's proper role in the global war, she continued to support China in its struggle against Japanese aggression. She had long been active as a propagandist and fund-raiser, especially for medical relief. In the summer of and fall of 1940, she led a campaign called 'The Book of Hope,' with a target of $100,000 for hospital supplies and equipment. Pearl raised the money by soliciting $100 contributions from one thousand women, each of whom also signed their name in an ornate book."

One of the women that Pearl S. Buck invited to join in this cause was a prominent Latter-day Saint who had been a vocal proponent of women's rights and health care for children, two causes that Pearl Buck ardently supported. In a letter dated 8 July 1940, Buck wrote:

"On July 7th of this year China commemorated the third anniversary of the Japanese invasion. For three years the people of China have endured and resisted with all their strength the same forces which are now devastating Europe. . . .

"In recognition of this brave spirit, I am inviting you to join a group of one thousand American women who wish to express their sympathy for the women of China who, throughout these terrible years of unspeakably barbaric invasion, have won the respect of all the world. . . . The gift itself will be more than a gesture of mercy and humanity. It will provide treatment for at least 800,000 of the most serious cases. But more than that, it will be a stimulus to the morale of the entire Chinese nation, fighting against such overwhelming odds to hold its own."

Pearl S. Buck added that she was appealing only "to outstanding women of known human sympathy." The recipient of the letter certainly met such a qualification. In May 1948, for example, the *Improvement Era* noted that she had donated $100 to Primary Children's Hospital. She became well known for her service to the young women of the Church. In addition, she attended the temple virtually every week for thirty years.

Affectionately known as "Aunt Augusta," Augusta ("Gusta") Winters Grant was married for sixty years to Heber J. Grant, who served as president of the Church for twenty-six years. Known for her unpretentious charm, Gusta accompanied her husband on visits to three U.S. presidents—Warren G. Harding, Calvin Coolidge, and Herbert Hoover—greatly improving the public image of the Church. Not coincidentally, 1930–40 was the first decade that positive articles about the Church outnumbered negative ones. The Word of Wisdom and the Church welfare program both received favorable attention.

When Pearl S. Buck was nine years old and living in China, Heber J. Grant made his own pilgrimage to the Far East, where he opened the first mission in Japan in 1901. The work was largely unsuccessful; he returned after two years and as president of the Church in 1924 closed the Japan Mission. Missionaries did not return to Japan until 1948, when the work flourished. Serviceman Boyd K. Packer performed one of the first baptisms in Japan after the war.

By the summer of 1942, Japan had conquered much of the Pacific—from the tip of the Aleutian Islands in the north to the Marshall and Gilbert Islands in the south; virtually all of Asia, including Java, Borneo, Sumatra, Malaya, Burma, Thailand, French Indochina, the Philippines, Hong Kong, Formosa, Manchuria; and key parts of Pearl S. Buck's beloved China, which would reel under Japanese domination for eight years, until Japan surrendered in the fall of 1945.

Throughout World War II and afterwards, Pearl S. Buck, author of more than seventy books and winner of the Nobel and Pulitzer Prizes, continued her advocacy for the poor, the persecuted, the disabled, and the disenfranchised. During the war, she spoke out against the internment of Japanese-Americans. She actively supported the civil rights movement. In 1949 she established Welcome House, the first international, interracial adoption agency, which has assisted in the adoption of more than six thousand children. In 1950 she published *The Child Who Never Grew* about her retarded daughter, Carol. The book changed American attitudes toward mental illness and was a key factor in Rose Kennedy's decision to speak publicly about her retarded child, Rosemary. Pearl S. Buck and her second husband, Richard Walsh, adopted six children.

Gusta patiently cared for President Grant after he had a series of strokes in the early 1940s. He died on 14 May 1945, one week after Germany surrendered.

After Heber's death, Gusta faithfully attended general conference, but at the October 1950 conference, President George Albert Smith noted her absence: "I also wish to mention Sister Augusta Grant. She has always been here when it was possible for her to do so. It is not possible for her to be out of the house and I am sure we all remember her as one of the lovely souls who have given cheer wherever they have gone. She is way past ninety years of age and I presume we might expect she would not have much strength at that age." After witnessing the trials and progress of the Church in much of two centuries, Gusta Grant died on 1 June 1952, at age ninety-five.

HOSTING
NIKITA KHRUSHCHEV

The son of a poor peasant farmer, Nikita Sergeyevich Khrushchev joined the Russian Bolsheviks (Communists) in 1918, the year after the Russian Revolution. Over the next two decades he gained favor with Communist officials and became a member of the ruling *politburo* in 1939. After Hitler invaded the Ukraine, then part of the Soviet Union, Khrushchev organized troops to battle the Germans and also led the effort to get Ukrainian farms, mines, and factories back into production. Khrushchev continued to gain power and was even bold enough to harshly criticize Stalin (who had died in 1953) for his crimes against the Soviet people. Such criticism gained acceptance, and in the resulting movement known as *de-Stalinization*, cities were renamed and statues destroyed. Nikita Khrushchev became premier of the Soviet Union in 1958 at the age of sixty-four.

One year later Khrushchev made an official trip to the United States, and an LDS government official was asked to supervise a tour that was part of the visit. Khrushchev, who at times could be surly and at other times good-natured, joked with the three hundred reporters accompanying him. At one point he said to the LDS brother, "Your grandchildren will live under communism."

"On the contrary," came the reply, "my grandchildren will live in freedom as I hope that all people will."

"Americans are so gullible," argued Khrushchev. "They are in the process of being fed small bits of socialism and one day will awaken to find themselves living under a totalitarian order."

On the return trip, the LDS official's adult son rode in a car with

Mrs. Khrushchev, her son-in-law (editor Alexi Adzhubei), two of her children, Mrs. Andrei Gromyko, and a translator. The son asked what they thought of the great Russian novelist Leo Tolstoy, and they responded enthusiastically. He then mentioned Tolstoy's reported comment to the president of Cornell University that "if Mormonism is able to endure unmodified until it reaches the third and fourth generation, it is destined to become the greatest power the world has ever known."

The group responded, "Tolstoy wrote much better than he spoke."

The son next told of Christ's original church, the apostasy, and the restoration, and his remarks stirred interest. When Mrs. Gromyko asked if he believed in God, he responded affirmatively, explaining the LDS belief in the Godhead and bearing his testimony of the Book of Mormon. He then persuaded the group to accept copies of the Book of Mormon (which were delivered on a later trip).

Many years later, F. Enzio Busche (born in Germany and sustained to the First Quorum of the Seventy in 1977) told Elder Benson that Alexi Adzhubei had visited German journalist Lambart Lensing after returning from America. Elder Busche related: "Mr. Lensing told me later, knowing that I was a Mormon, that Alexi Adzhubei mentioned to him that America as a whole did not impress him very much and that the only thing that touched him deeply was the Mormons and their philosophy of life."

Although he said his enthusiasm for hosting Khrushchev could have been put "in a small thimble," Ezra Taft Benson did so as part of his duties as Secretary of Agriculture under President Dwight Eisenhower. (His son Reed Benson had the discussion with Mrs. Khrushchev's party regarding LDS doctrine.) Brother Benson took Khrushchev on a tour of the U.S. Department of Agriculture Beltsville Experiment Station in Maryland, saying in his opening remarks, "Under our capitalistic free enterprise system [our farmers] have developed an agriculture unequaled anywhere in the world."

Khrushchev, who had initiated Soviet programs to increase the production of grain, scoffed at the station, saying, "We do better than this" and "I know all about this," even though he and Elder Benson, who had been a member of the Quorum of the Twelve since 1943, both knew U.S. methods were clearly more productive.

Just a week after Khrushchev's visit, Secretary Benson departed with his wife, Flora, his daughters Beverly and Bonnie, and four staff members for a tour of seven European countries, including the Soviet Union. The party was well received in Moscow, staying at the prestigious Sovietskaya Hotel and attending a performance at the Bolshoi Theater. Ezra also wanted to visit one of the two Protestant churches in the city but received no cooperation from Soviet officials. Finally, as they left for the airport, Ezra made the request again. This time it was inexplicably granted.

An American newsman wrote, "Every face in the old [Baptist] sanctuary gaped incredulously as our obviously American group was led down the aisle. They grabbed for our hands as we proceeded to our pews which were gladly vacated. . . . Their wrinkled old faces looked at us pleadingly. They reached out to touch us almost as one would reach out for the last final caress of one's most-beloved just before the casket is lowered. They were in misery and yet a light shone through the misery. They gripped our hands like frightened children."

An official further surprised Elder Benson by asking him to speak. His emotions close to the surface, he talked of the Savior's love. "Jesus Christ, the Redeemer of the World, watches over this earth. . . . Be unafraid, keep His commandments, love one another, pray for peace, and all will be well."

"*Ja, ja, ja!*" responded the Russian women.

"I leave you my witness as a church servant for many years that the truth will endure," continued Elder Benson. "Time is on the side of truth. God bless you and keep you all the days of your life."

Both the speaker and the congregation were now in tears. Many waved handkerchiefs and grasped his hand. Then they began singing in Russian, "God Be with You Till We Meet Again."

"I shall never forget that evening as long as I live," recalled Elder Benson. "Seldom, if ever, have I felt the oneness of mankind and the unquenchable yearning of the human heart for freedom."

Reporter Grant Salisbury wrote in the 26 October 1959 edition of *U.S. News and World Report,* "It turned out to be one of the most moving experiences in the lifetime of many of us. One newsman, a former Marine, ranked it with the sight of the American flag rising over the old American compound in Tientsin, China, at the end of World War II."

A VISIT FROM
JANE ADDAMS

Born of Quaker parents in 1860, Jane Addams was drawn to social causes from a young age. On a trip to Europe in the 1880s, she visited London's Toynbee Hall, the first of many "settlement houses," which were institutions established to improve living conditions in inner cities. Toynbee Hall offered recreational, cultural, and educational activities. Addams began formulating plans to set up a settlement house in the United States, and in 1889 she and Ellen Gates Starr founded Hull House in Chicago. It began in a rundown mansion originally owned by Chicago businessman Charles Hull.

Hull House social efforts included helping many foreign-born immigrants learn English, instituting programs to prevent juvenile delinquency, and providing a spectrum of activities for the poor, from drama and music to sports and crafts. By 1907 Hull House had expanded to twelve buildings. Jane Addams also campaigned for woman suffrage and lectured widely on such topics as child labor, public health, housing reform, and unemployment.

In 1902, a thirty-year-old Latter-day Saint woman arrived in Chicago, accompanying her husband, who was attending graduate school at the University of Chicago. She had shown a keen interest in education as a girl and attended Brigham Young Academy as a teenager, living with the Karl G. Maeser family. She later noted the influence of Brother Maeser (the founder of Brigham Young Academy), George H. Brimhall (president of Brigham Young University from 1900 to 1921), and Alice Louise Reynolds (the first female professor at BYU). When this young woman graduated at age eighteen,

Brother Maeser put her in charge of the Primary department, where she taught for four years. She then taught elementary school in Salt Lake City.

With her husband studying engineering, this sister began taking classes in social work. In her words, "While studying at the University of Chicago, I attended a number of [Jane Addams's] lectures at Hull House, and upon assignment from my professor, I spent several days at this famous settlement to obtain material for a term paper. She gave me the privilege of several personal interviews. I visited Hull House again in 1911 with . . . delegates to the National Council meeting in Chicago, and we were luncheon guests of Miss Addams in the famous Hull House dining room."

A memorable moment in this LDS sister's association with Addams came many years later:

"Jane Addams, the great social pioneer, writer, lecturer, peace advocate, founder of the famous social settlement, Hull House, was in her lifetime known the world over as America's most revered woman. One lovely summer morning I went down to the office [in the Relief Society Building] early to complete an important piece of work, and as I sat down at my desk alone I heard someone walk gently down the hall into the outer office. I looked up and there in the doorway, bare-headed, stood the famous and lovely Jane Addams. Not feeling well, she had stopped in Salt Lake City for a day or so on a return trip from California. While her traveling companion made a side trip to Yellowstone Park, she was resting at the Hotel Utah. She said that upon learning that she was so near the Relief Society office she had decided to walk over since she had always admired the work of this organization and the splendid service it has given, and she added, 'I value highly my acquaintance with my Mormon friends.' She remained for over an hour, manifesting keen interest in our work and our plans."

Amy Brown Lyman, wife of apostle Richard R. Lyman, was pro-
foundly affected by her visits to Hull House and her interviews with
Jane Addams. "It was at this time that I first became interested in
social work and social problems," she later wrote. "Through a former
Michigan classmate of my husband, who was then working in the
Chicago Charities, I was invited to do volunteer social work in this
agency. These experiences . . . were all profitable and started me on my
way as a social worker."

Indeed, she became an outstanding social worker in her own right.
She served as the first director of the Church Social Welfare
Department, which helped women and couples with such crucial issues
as employment, adoption, and education. She also organized programs
to train Relief Society volunteers in welfare and medical principles. As
a member of the Utah State legislature, she helped pass legislation
related to maternity and infant care. She donated her time and talents
to the Salt Lake City Community Clinic, the National Conference of
Social Workers, the National Conference of Charities and Correction,
the American Association for Mental Deficiency, and many other
charitable institutions.

During this entire period Sister Lyman also carried heavy Relief
Society responsibilities, first as a member of the general board (1909),
then general secretary (1913), editor of the *Relief Society Magazine*
(1921), and first counselor to general president Louise Y. Robison
(1928). In 1940 she became general president of the Relief Society.
Her administration organized Relief Society projects to stock Church
welfare storehouses and to assist the Red Cross during World War II.
By the time of her release in 1945, she had served thirty-six years in
the general Relief Society.

In her autobiography entitled *In Retrospect*, Amy Brown Lyman paid tribute to Jane Addams, noting that "this visit to our office was the highlight of my acquaintance with Jane Addams, and it was a great honor for the Relief Society to have as a visitor this distinguished woman who has been called the 'best beloved woman in America' and the greatest woman of her time.

"The name of Jane Addams is always included in any list of great American women, and usually stands first. Dr. Emil Ludwig, the historian and biographic appraiser of reputations, stated, in 1928, that the four greatest living Americans in their order were: Thomas A. Edison, Jane Addams, John D. Rockefeller, and Orville Wright. Ida M. Tarbell, in 1930, listed Jane Adams among the fifty living women who had done most to advance the welfare of the United States; and, in 1933, she was one of the twelve American women chosen by the women of America in a nationwide poll as the great women leaders of the past century. Miss Addams's dying words were: 'Don't think of me in veneration, but carry on my humanitarian work.'"

Jane Addams died in 1935 at age seventy-five, continuing her service at Hull House right up to her death.

Amy Brown Lyman died on 5 December 1959 at age eighty-seven. "My testimony has been my anchor and my stay," she wrote, "my satisfaction in times of joy and gladness, my comfort in times of discouragement."

MEETING EINSTEIN
AT PRINCETON

~~~~~~><~~~~~~

Born in Germany in 1879, Albert Einstein showed streaks of brilliance as a boy and taught himself Euclidean geometry at the age of twelve. At the same time, he was not interested in his school classes, withdrawing from school at age fifteen. He eventually completed secondary school in Switzerland and then entered the Swiss National Polytechnic, where he frequently skipped classes to study on his own or play his violin. His professors did not recommend him for a university position, and by 1902 Albert was working as an examiner in a Swiss patent office.

Over the next fifteen years he received a doctorate at the University of Zurich and began to publish highly influential physics papers. He wrote on such topics as the nature of light, electromagnetic radiation, and the electrodynamics of moving bodies. He became best known, however, for his special and general theories of relativity. The special theory holds that an observer at rest and an observer moving at a uniform speed will experience the same laws of mechanics and that light has a uniform velocity. The general theory postulates that gravity and acceleration both have the same result.

By 1920 Einstein had become famous throughout the world; he received the Nobel Prize for Physics in 1922. He traveled widely and was continually followed by photographers, becoming the most famous scientist of the twentieth century. He continued to live in Europe, but when Hitler rose to power in 1933, Einstein accepted a position with the Institute for Advanced Study in Princeton, New Jersey. The Institute was a sort of intellectual monastery that allowed a group of scholars to freely study, debate ideas, and conduct experiments with-out specific deadlines or other pressures. Einstein, who was fifty-four when he came to New Jersey, flourished in this atmosphere and became quite popular.

A Latter-day Saint scholar and scientist had been teaching at Princeton University for two years when Einstein arrived. Twenty-two years younger than Einstein, he had received a Ph.D. in chemistry from Berkeley when he was twenty-six. He published many important papers and became one of the most respected chemists in the country. He and his family lived in Princeton until 1946, where Einstein remained until his death in 1955.

Many years later, this LDS brother was asked about his view of Einstein.

"He was first rate, there is no question about it," replied the LDS scholar. "It was no accident that he was good in many fields, but the picture some people have of him as a lone intellectual giant is a wrong one. I prefer to think of him as a man with few peers. There are other people who are comparable. Neils Bohr was another physicist of comparable scientific influence."

The man further noted that Einstein did not get the Nobel Prize for the theory of relativity but for the photoelectric effect. "The photo-electric effect has to do with the emission of electrons when a ray of light strikes certain chemicals. And the color of the light determines the speed at which the electron will come out."

Over his distinguished career, LDS scientist Henry Eyring received many awards, including the National Medal of Science and the Medal of the Swedish Academy (which is awarded only once every fifty years). He also served as a branch president, district president, and member of the general board of the Sunday School.

Serving as district president while at Princeton, Henry Eyring joked that he presided over three million people, "though most of them were blissfully unaware of the fact." Among those three million were Einstein, and, judging from the stories told about him at Princeton, he was Henry Eyring's kind of man. Shortly after arriving at a home temporarily rented for him, for instance, Einstein changed into casual clothes and ventured down Nassau Street to buy an ice cream cone and mingle with the university students. Not long after that, when asked at a dinner what historical person he would most like to meet, Einstein chose Moses: "I would like to ask him if he ever thought that his people would obey his law so long."

One former student told another story that typified Professor Eyring's humor and spunk. When the student arrived to take his oral examinations, Henry was the only committee member who had arrived. Wanting to help the student relax, he asked if he had ever seen him jump to the table from a standing position. "No," replied the student, at which Brother Eyring jumped, failing in his attempt and striking his shins against the side of the table. "For a few moments I thought the oral would have to be canceled," recalled the student, "but with pain and determination he backed off and tried it again, this time succeeding."

Interestingly, Henry Eyring's son Henry B. Eyring, who was called as an apostle in 1995, was born in Princeton on 31 May 1933, just a few months before Einstein arrived.

A GIFT FOR
DWIGHT EISENHOWER

During his second term as president of the United States, Dwight Eisenhower invited an LDS couple who were friends of his to a White House dinner. After the dinner, the president greeted ambassadors and other dignitaries in a reception line. Then he crossed the large room to talk to the LDS couple, discussing grandchildren and one of the president's favorite pastimes—hunting. The couple invited the president to their country estate, and he accepted. The visit was scheduled for November 1959.

Preparing for the president's visit, the husband had all the barns on the farm painted. Then he purchased a special Christmas gift for Eisenhower: a 20-gauge mahogany-stocked Browning shotgun. But Mr. Eisenhower came down with a serious cold and sent word to the couple that he regretfully had to cancel his trip. When he left on a three-week, eleven-nation tour early in December, the couple concluded they would have no chance to see him before Christmas.

On 22 December, however, the president's appointment secretary called and asked if the husband could be at the White House the next morning. "The president would like to see you," he said. The LDS brother arrived the next morning with several boxes of candy and the president's shotgun. Eisenhower was delighted with the gift, and the two of them spent fifteen minutes in the oval office assembling the gun. The president then practiced putting it together himself. Then, holding the gun to his shoulder, he followed an imaginary pheasant through the windows of the oval office.

"He was like a little boy with a new toy," recalled the brother.

Although he had expected to wish the president a merry Christmas, chat for a minute, and promptly leave, J. Willard Marriott spent forty-five minutes with Dwight David Eisenhower ("Ike") that day. Commenting on the shotgun, Eisenhower said, "It's light and it's a beauty. I'll take it to Augusta with me and have the caddy strap it to my golf bag. We're always flushing out quail down there."

The two of them also reminisced about simpler times. In 1933, a decade before he became a national hero, Ike had accepted a post in the nation's capital as aide to General Douglas MacArthur. Ike and his wife Mamie, who had grown to love Mexican food while stationed in San Antonio, Texas, had gone at least once a week to the Connecticut Avenue Hot Shoppe restaurant for chili and hot tamales. Brother Marriott and his wife Alice Sheets Marriott ("Allie") had founded the Hot Shoppe chain when they had virtually nothing. They had launched their business with a $200 cash reserve, and their first restaurant had been a small root beer stand.

"Could Mamie and I get some [chili and hot tamales] sent into the White House, so we could have a real oldtime Mexican [dinner]?" asked the president.

"Anytime you want, Mr. President. Just say the word."

In the hectic election year that followed, however, the request never came.

Succeeded in the White House by John F. Kennedy, Ike left public office in 1961. He and Mamie retired to their farm in Gettysburg, Pennsylvania, the first home they had ever owned. The former president, who had grown up in Abilene, Kansas, raised cattle and published three books of memoirs. He suffered a series of heart attacks and died in a Washington, D.C., hospital on 28 March 1969. He was seventy-eight.

A FRIENDSHIP WITH SUSAN B. ANTHONY

Like the great social reformer Jane Addams, Susan B. Anthony was born of Quaker parents who believed in equal education for girls. After teaching school as a young woman, Susan joined the temperance movement. She frequently found, however, that women were ignored at temperance meetings. At a New York rally in 1852, she was not allowed to speak because she was a woman. Such experiences sparked a concern for society's treatment of women, and she soon joined with Elizabeth Cady Stanton in a fifty-year fight for women's rights.

As Anthony and Stanton's national women's movement gained momentum in the 1870s, Utah women, who had been given state voting rights in 1870, were campaigning for national rights as well. *Woman's Exponent* was an independent newspaper that published articles, stories, poems, and editorials on "every subject as it arises in which the women of Utah . . . are specifically interested." In 1877 an LDS woman became editor of the *Exponent* and wrote editorials on woman suffrage and equality for women in other areas.

In 1879, this editor and Zina Young Williams attended a meeting of the National Woman Suffrage Association (NWSA). Susan B. Anthony was impressed with her abilities, and the two became friends. Three years later, the editor spoke at an NWSA conference. Over the next two decades she held important positions in the Suffrage Association, the National Council of Women, and the International Council of Women. In 1895 she was among a group of LDS women who hosted a visit by Susan B. Anthony to Salt Lake City.

As editor of *Woman's Exponent* for thirty-seven years, Emmeline B. Wells championed a multitude of women's and Relief Society causes, maintaining a positive relationship with national women leaders. In 1899, Emmeline attended the Women's International Council and Congress, where she met Queen Victoria. "I desire," wrote Emmeline, "to do all in my power to help elevate the condition of my own people, especially women."

Among Church leaders who actively supported woman suffrage were Brigham Young, George Q. Cannon, Orson F. Whitney, and Heber J. Grant. (B. H. Roberts, by contrast, opposed voting rights for women on the basis that they would harm themselves if they entered "the filthy stream of politics.")

When Susan B. Anthony visited Salt Lake City in 1895, Heber J. Grant, then a junior apostle, recorded: "This evening Gusta and I attended the meeting held in the interests of the Woman's suffrage cause in the Assembly Hall. Susan B. Anthony, Rev. Anna Shaw and others addressed the meeting. I was pleased with all that was said, but was amused beyond expression by Miss Shaw's address. It was brim full and running over with good things and delivered with force and ability. She has a very amusing way of telling things and I do not think that I ever laughed so much in a half hour before in my life as I did when she was showing up some of the absurdities of those opposed to woman's suffrage."

In 1920, Emmeline B. Wells was ninety years old and serving in her final year as general Relief Society president when the Nineteenth Amendment to the U.S. Constitution was finally passed, giving national voting rights to women. Her friend Susan B. Anthony had died fourteen years earlier.

A National Hero
Defends the Church

Although Wilford Woodruff's 1890 Manifesto had signaled the end of plural marriage, controversy continued to surround the Church in the early twentieth century. The mainstream press viciously attacked the Church and distorted its doctrines. When apostle Reed Smoot was elected to the U.S. Senate in 1903, a national controversy erupted over whether he should be allowed to keep his seat. While Smoot retained his place in the Senate, the controversy continued.

In 1911, *Collier's* magazine published a letter from an enormously popular national hero. The letter, which ran more than 2,500 words, defended Senator Smoot and the Church. Speaking of Reed Smoot, the writer noted, " . . . it was the universal testimony of all who knew anything of his domestic life that it was exemplary in every way. He also assured me that he had always done everything he could to have the law about polygamy absolutely obeyed, and most strongly upheld the position that the Church had taken in its public renunciation of polygamy, and that he would act as quickly against any Mormon who nowadays made a plural marriage as against a Gentile who committed bigamy. I looked into the facts very thoroughly, became convinced that Senator Smoot had told me the truth, and treated him exactly as I did all other Senators—that is, strictly on his merits as a public servant."

This well-known and well-respected man went on to say "that if Mr. Smoot or any one else had disobeyed the law he should, of course, be turned out, but if he had obeyed the law and was an upright and reputable man in his public and private relations, it would be an outrage to turn him out because of his religious belief."

Although he was only fifty-two when he wrote this letter, Teddy Roosevelt had already completed his eight-year tenure as president of the United States. Elected vice president in 1900, he was forty-two—and the youngest man to become chief executive—when he became president at the assassination of William McKinley. Roosevelt initially believed Reed Smoot should be denied his seat in the Senate, but as the two men became better acquainted, they became allies. Roosevelt showed Apostle Smoot's impact on him when he wrote, "I have known monogamous Mormons whose standard of domestic life and morality and whose attitude toward the relations of men and women was as high as that of the best citizens of any other creed; indeed, among these Mormons the standard of sexual morality was unusually high."

When he was twenty-one, Teddy had married eighteen-year-old Alice Hathaway Lee. Four years later, she gave birth to a daughter but died two days later. On the same day—14 February 1884—Teddy's mother died of typhoid fever. The young man, who had already begun a political career, took his daughter west and settled in the Dakota Territory. He recovered from the double tragedy by working long hours on his ranch and by writing books about the American West. He even assisted law officers in tracking down a band of outlaws.

When Teddy lost most of his cattle to a series of blizzards, he returned to New York City and the political life. He rose steadily, and when William McKinley was elected president in 1896, he appointed Roosevelt as assistant secretary of the Navy. When the Spanish-American War broke out in 1898, however, Roosevelt resigned and recruited cowboys and athletes to fight the Spanish in Cuba. He led his "rough riders" to an impressive victory at San Juan Hill, and twenty years later reflected, "San Juan was the great day of my life."

"Ye That Embark in the Service of God": Living and Preaching the Gospel

"ONE OF THE DEAREST FRIENDS WE WILL EVER KNOW"

By the time World War II ended in Europe in early May of 1945, more than ten million civilians had been killed in the countries of Germany, Poland, Yugoslavia, Romania, France, and Hungary. In Holland alone, where more than 200,000 people died, almost half a million homes had been destroyed or damaged, thousands of farms had been ruined, and forty percent of the livestock had been lost. Bridges, highways, and railroads had been destroyed throughout Europe. As a result, millions of Europeans were thrust into poverty, many of them threatened with starvation.

George Albert Smith, who was ordained president of the Church two weeks after the war ended, was deeply concerned about the situation in Europe and approached United States president Harry S Truman about the possibility of sending aid. Later he recalled:

"When the war was over, I went representing the Church, to see the president of the United States. When I called on him, he received me very graciously—I had met him before—and I said: 'I have just come to ascertain from you, Mr. President, what your attitude will be if the Latter-day Saints are prepared to ship food and clothing and bedding to Europe.'

"He smiled and looked at me, and said: 'Well, what do you want to ship it over there for? Their money isn't any good.'

"I said: 'We don't want their money.' He looked at me and asked: 'You don't mean you are going to give it to them?'

"I said: 'Of course, we would give it to them. They are our brothers and sisters and are in distress. God has blessed us with a surplus, and we will be glad to send it if we can have the co-operation of the government.'

"He said: 'You are on the right track,' and added, 'we will be glad to help you in any way we can.'"

With the way cleared, the Church president urged members of the Church in the United States to help their fellow Saints in Europe. In response, Church members sent clothing, shoes, bedding, and food. Relief Society sisters had already donated two thousand quilts. Volunteers flooded Welfare Square to pack thousands of boxes and type shipping labels. Items had to be sent in small packages since government regulations prohibited boxes heavier than eleven pounds.

Goods sent to Europe included the following:

- 2,342,000 pounds of wheat products
- 1,114,000 pounds of clothing, shoes, and coats
- 2,600,000 pounds of fruit, vegetables, and milk
- 400,000 pounds of meat products
- 200,000 pounds of dry beans

Ezra Taft Benson, a junior member of the Quorum of the Twelve Apostles, was assigned to travel to Europe and supervise welfare work there. Elder Benson departed in January of 1946 with Frederick W. Babbel, a recently returned German-speaking missionary, accompanying him as aide and secretary. A month later, four boxcars of food and clothing left Salt Lake City for New York, to then be shipped to Europe.

By June of 1946, the first shipments arrived in Geneva, Switzerland. Elder Benson later recalled, "One of the happiest days of my life was that day when the first supplies arrived in Berlin." When Elder Benson took acting mission president Richard Ranglack to see the commodities, President Ranglack was incredulous. "Do you mean to tell me those boxes are full of food?"

"Yes," replied Elder Benson, "food, clothing, bedding, and a few medical supplies."

After they opened several boxes and examined the precious wheat, beans, and other supplies, a grateful President Ranglack said through his tears, "Brother Benson, it is hard for me to believe that people who have never seen us could do so much for us."

Witnessing miracle after miracle, Elders Benson and Babbel served the European Saints for almost a year. Back at home, Elder Benson's family witnessed their own miracle. Elder and Sister Benson's little daughter was gravely ill. Elder Benson was hundreds of miles away, and Sister Benson was left to care for and comfort the girl alone. One night an apostle came to their home and blessed the baby that she would be healed. Elder Benson later recalled:

"I shall never cease to be grateful for the visits he made to my home while I was serving as a humble missionary in the nations of war-torn Europe at the end of World War II. Particularly am I thankful for a visit in the still of the night when our little one lay at death's door. Without any announcement, [he] found time to come into that home and place his hands upon the head of that little one, held in her mother's arms as she had been for many hours, and promise her complete recovery. . . . He always had time to help, particularly those who were sick, those who needed him most."

It was Church president George Albert Smith who visited Harry Truman in 1945 on behalf of the Saints to offer aid after the War. He had assigned Ezra Taft Benson to serve in Europe, and it was this same man, George Albert Smith, who blessed Elder Benson's child when she lay at death's door.

In providing relief to victims of the war in Europe, Church members sent approximately 7,000 boxes of food, clothing, and bedding—the equivalent of 133 boxcar loads. The first shipments went to Denmark, France, Belgium, Norway, and other countries in western Europe. Later, largely due to the efforts of Ezra Taft Benson and Frederick Babbel, shipments to Germany, Austria, and Czechoslovakia were possible.

After forty tons of wheat sent by the Church arrived in Greece, Archbishop Athenagoris, national chairman of the Greek War Relief Association, sent the following message to Church headquarters:

"Yours is a gift which will bring comfort and relief to thousands of hungry Greeks and it will be all the more welcome representing as it does the compassionate sympathy of our Christian brothers in America."

The message was received by George Albert Smith. His unpublicized, loving visits to those struggling with difficulties were not uncommon. President Smith died on 4 April 1951, his eighty-first birthday.

Days later, at General Conference, Apostle John A. Widtsoe related an experience quite similar to Elder Benson's:

"During the events of the last few days, many memories have crowded in upon my mind. In a late afternoon of a warm, sultry day in August or September, I sat in my office rather tired after the day's work. The University of Utah had had internal dissensions which had been fanned by enemies into a nationwide scandal. I had been called in to assist others who were trying to return the institution and its work to a normal condition. It was the third time in my life that I had been obliged to serve my state in such a capacity. I was weary. Just then there was a knock upon the door, and in walked George Albert Smith. He said, 'I am on the way home after my day's work. I thought of you and the problems that you are expected to solve. I came in to comfort you and to bless you.'

"That was the way of George Albert Smith. Of the many friends I have throughout the state and beyond, he was the only one, except a few of my intimate friends, who took time to give me the loving help in the work I had to do. Of course I appreciated that; I shall never forget it. We talked together for awhile; we parted, he went home. My heart was lifted. I was weary no longer."

At the invitation of President David O. McKay, Sister Irene Jones, of the Society For the Aid of the Sightless, also paid tribute to George Albert Smith at the conference: "Through the loving spirit of President George Albert Smith, the work for the blind in the Church has expanded, and reached out to touch the lives and enrich the lives of Latter-day Saints and Gentiles. He believed in us and, because of that faith, we have learned to believe in ourselves and have been brought by a way we knew not.

"Even in his illness he did not forget us, but sent messages of encouragement and inspiration by his secretary and daughters.

"Wednesday, April 4, 1951, was a dark day in the lives of the blind, for we feel that we have lost one of the dearest friends we will ever know, and one of the greatest humanitarians that ever lived. For consolation I have played the record of his dear voice, which he gave me at Christmas time, and, as I listened, I felt that he was very near and that he would always be close at hand to guide us."

Telling the Story of Brigham Young

Shortly before her death in 1965 at age ninety-one, a granddaughter of Brigham Young reminisced about her mother in an interview: "Mother, when she was a very young woman, said that she would like to write the life of her father [Brigham Young]. Well, I was born when Mother was sixteen. When Mother was seventeen I was two months old, so as I grew we became more like sisters rather than mother and daughter, and having always had good training, I always helped her with her writing. And she would gather, wherever she could find anything about her father—she'd put it in a book or a manuscript she was keeping and said someday she'd write a book.

"I noticed at one time she quit writing about her father, and I said, 'Mother, what are you doing about your book? I never hear you talk about writing any more.'

"She said, 'I can't write about Brigham Young—he's too big for me. I'm not big enough to understand him. How can you describe a mountain when you're standing under it? You have to get away from it to see it.'

"I said, 'Nevertheless, you've got to write that book, you're the only one of his children who can write it, or who will write it, and you have to do it.'

"'Well,' she said, 'I don't know how.'

"I said, 'You keep at it and whenever you think of anything or hear of anything about your father, you write it down. And then someday I'll help you organize it.' And when she had her manuscript all together in those two big books, I took hold of it, and for my spare time—I was a busy wife of a college president for many years of my life—I would go up to Mother's and get busy with her manuscript and finally I organized the book *Brigham Young* in chapters and gathered her material together under each chapter so that it was in rather presentable shape.

"Then one day an English traveler [Harold Shepstone] came to Utah who was a newspaper representative for half a dozen newspapers in Great Britain. . . . He met my mother and became fascinated with her as people usually did, for Mother was a very charming conversationalist, and Mother told him about her book, and he said, 'Let me see your manuscript . . .' So Mother took her manuscript down to him, and he gave it back to her with the opinion that it was very promising, and he thought it would make a most interesting reading. . . . That was the year that my husband was appointed as president of the European Missions and I told my hubby when were packing, getting ready to go, that I was going to take my book . . . and look up Shepstone . . . to see if he would be interested in making a book out of it—printing it—which I did. So I sent the book to Shepstone, and he asked permission to write a number of articles from the manuscripts for the Sunday newspapers over in England . . . [and] his work was very acceptable, and finally he asked permission to make a book out of it, which was gladly given him.

"The book was finally printed in England, at Jarrolds, one of the finest printing establishments in all England. It sold many editions in England . . . and I think it was the first book, one of the first, anyway, that was printed in the East or abroad without a Church guarantee of taking 1,000 copies in return for its printing. It had no guarantee whatever from the Church, but the Jerrolds people were so sure of its success that they gave Mother $500 before it was printed. . . . Unfortunately, the book is now out of print, but it is one of the finest histories of Brigham Young, his life and times. I wish it were in print today."

The mother and daughter were Susa Young Gates and Leah Eudora Dunford Widtsoe, both accomplished writers. Their book, *The Life Story of Brigham Young*, was published in 1930 in England, where Leah served as president of the Relief Societies of the European Mission and her husband, John A. Widtsoe, as president of the European Mission.

Susa was born in 1856 to Brigham Young and Lucy Bigelow. Her private education included music and ballet, and she entered the University of Deseret at age thirteen. While there, she co-edited the *College Lantern*, possibly the first college newspaper in the western United States. Susa described herself thus: "5'3". 115 lbs. Dark blue or grey eyes, light 'rather curly' brown hair. I must confess my teeth are the only redeeming feature of my face."

Recalling her father, she said he amused babies with a "too-roo-loo-rool-lool-or-loo" that would always "dry up any incipient torrent on a baby's cheek." She also noted his kindness and attention toward child visitors bringing messages from their parents.

Not surprisingly, Brigham could be suspicious of his daughters' male companions.

"On one occasion," wrote Susa, "just as [Brigham] was stepping into his carriage, he saw a strange young man about to enter the house gate. Instantly the flood of usual questions was poured out upon the embarrassed youth. Apparently not quite satisfied with the answers given, father asked, abruptly:

"'Are you a Mormon?'

"'Well,' floundered the lad, 'slightly.'

"Father burst into his quiet, mellow laugh. . . ."

At age sixteen, Susa married St. George dentist Alma Dunford; they had two children, Leah and Alma. Susa and Alma Sr. were divorced five years later, and he raised the children. Susa married Jacob F. Gates in 1880; she later founded the *Young Woman's Journal* and the *Relief Society Magazine* and served as press chairman of the National Council of Women.

During her fascinating life, Susa experienced a number of firsts:

She was the first person born in the Lion House.

She was the first person baptized for the dead in the St. George Temple.

She was the first (and only) woman to have an office in the Church Administration Building at 47 East South Temple.

Leah Dunford Widtsoe was born in 1874, three years before her grandfather Brigham Young died. When former Brigham Young University president Franklin S. Harris spoke at John A. Widtsoe's funeral in 1952, he paid this tribute to Sister Widtsoe: "We have never ceased to marvel at the resourcefulness of Aunt Leah, as we affectionately call her, and we soon became aware of one of the chief sources of the strength of this great man. She has supported him without reserve and he constantly relied on her judgment, particularly in the work for women and in the extension activities which he initiated in all three of Utah's institutions of higher learning."

FOUR DECADES
OF SERVICE

A general president of the Relief Society served faithfully despite turbulent social times and personal trials. During her tenure as president she lost her seventy-one-year-old husband and forty-year-old daughter within a fourteen-month period of time. When she was released as general president a decade later, she thus returned to an empty home. Alone and unable to sleep, she sat down at her typewriter and recorded her emotions, typing well into the night:

"While my body is tired, very tired, tonight as three days of intensive effort incident to a General Relief Society Conference comes to a close, and three sessions of General Church Conference with a 7:00 A.M. Welfare Meeting which took me from my home at 6:00 A.M. and at which I spoke, my spirit seems 'to reach the unreachable stars.' After 39½ years of service on the General Board of Relief Society, including eight years as Editor of The Relief Society Magazine . . . I was honored beyond my fondest dreams by the thoughtful and courteous attention given to my release as President of the Society and by the words of the Prophet . . . in commendation of my service to Relief Society and to organized non-Latter-day Saint women. . . . The response of the sisters of the Church to the announcement was one of 'startled surprise and disappointment.'

". . . The release was expected and very welcome, but the warmth of the response to my work was unexpected and will be a treasured memory forever. I felt the sincere love and appreciation of men and women with whom I have worked and whose regard I value and whom I esteem as the truly great of the earth.

"... Naturally my busy mind refuses to quit working as I lie here in bed physically tired. The lights are out, and it is time for sleep—'sleep that knits the raveled sleeve of care.' Yet that busy little mind says, 'Remember this! Remember that! why would you sleep when there has been so much that has been so glorious for you to review in memory?'

"At length I leave my bed to put in writing for my own future benefit my feelings at this time of release.

"There comes to my mind that day . . . when I sat in the conference room of the First Presidency in the Church Administration Building and was notified by the Brethren that the following day my name would be presented at a general Church conference session for a sustaining vote as the new general president of Relief Society. I sat in silent awe and wonder at being in the presence of the First Presidency and receiving through these Brethren such an 'honored calling from the Lord' which they referred to in these words. What was happening to me seemed unbelievable. The magnitude of the calling and a realization of my inadequacies swept through me, seeming to rob me of physical strength and voice. Anxiety as to my worthiness and to my ability to meet the requirements of the calling were co-mingled, but there was also a clear recognition that to question the wisdom of it was to question the inspiration of the Lord's chosen prophets. Humbly, I thanked the Brethren and said I would do my best with their help and guidance and that of the Lord. This I have conscientiously endeavored to do.

"... The Lord has been good to me! Many, many times he has put ideas into my mind and even words into my mouth that have enabled me to meet difficult situations or remove obstacles that otherwise might have impaired the work of the Society."

In her reminiscence, Belle S. Spafford noted that "Twenty-nine and a half years have passed since that day [of her calling], during which I have served under six of the Prophet-Presidents of the Church: Presidents Heber J. Grant, George Albert Smith, David O. McKay, Joseph Fielding Smith, Harold B. Lee and Spencer W. Kimball and their great and inspired counselors. What a rare and marvelous blessing!"

Sister Spafford thus served longer and under more Church presidents than any other general president of the Relief Society. (The president with the second longest term of service was Eliza R. Snow; she served twenty-one years.) When she was called in 1945, Sister Spafford selected Marianne Clark Sharp (daughter of J. Reuben Clark Jr.) as first counselor. The two served together until their release in 1974. (Gertrude Ryberg Garff, Velma Nebeker Simonsen, Helen Woodruff Anderson, and Louise Wallace Madsen served at different times as second counselor.)

One of Sister Spafford's first acts as president was to create a new and enlarged Relief Society social service and child welfare department. Throughout her administration, she emphasized adoption services and programs to guide youth and help abused children. Such concern with social issues carried on the tradition of Sister Spafford's predecessor, Amy Brown Lyman. It also brought Sister Spafford into national prominence. She was a member of the National Council of Women for forty-two years and served as president of that organization from 1968 to 1970.

On the day she was released, Sister Spafford wrote that "Elder Thomas Monson, Elder Marvin J. Ashton, and Elder Bruce R. McConkie attended the prayer meeting prior to the opening session of the Relief Society Conference. Their words were heartening beyond belief. Elder Boyd K. Packer spent an hour with me in my office the day before. What great and marvelous men to so honor me! All three members of the Presiding Bishopric [Presiding Bishop Victor L. Brown and counselors H. Burke Peterson and Vaughn J. Featherstone) made me feel they were suffering a severe loss in my release."

Released as general Relief Society president five days before she turned seventy-nine, Sister Spafford continued to serve in her ward Relief Society and in national organizations. The National Council of Women declared her eighty-fifth birthday "Belle S. Spafford Day," and when she retired from the council a year later, the Belle S. Spafford Archival Fellowship at New York University was formed.

Sister Spafford, who died at age eighty-six in 1982, offered a fitting epitaph to her Relief Society years—indeed, to a lifetime of service— when she wrote: "Today this office and calling was terminated by a prophet-president of the Church. A deep-seated feeling of gratitude engulfs me that I have been blessed and honored to have had such a glorious calling; that now my great mission is honorably completed, as attested by the Lord's prophets. A sweet feeling of relief and joy pervades my being that the responsibilities of this exacting calling have been placed on younger shoulders [the new president was Barbara B. Smith] whose responsibilities may differ with differing times, but whose calling is from the same divine source. There is within my soul a feeling of peace and good promise for the future—my personal future and that of my beloved Relief Society.

"I must write no more. Peace of mind which invokes sleep and rest are taking over. My busy mind seems to have grown drowsy and is going to sleep. Tonight I will rest for in my heart is the assurance that all is well."

"I Seemed to See
a Council in Heaven"

A young apostle experienced serious doubts about his own worthiness when he was called at age twenty-five. Remembering that difficult time, he wrote, "I have felt my own lack of ability. In fact when I was called as one of the Apostles I arose to my feet to say it was beyond anything I was worthy of, and as I was rising the thought came to me 'You know as you know that you live that John Taylor is a prophet of God, and to decline this office when he had received a revelation is equivalent to repudiating the Prophet.' I said, 'I will accept the office and do my best.' I remember that it was with difficulty that I took my seat without fainting.

"There are two spirits striving with us always, one telling us to continue our labor for good, and one telling us that with the faults and failings of our nature we are unworthy. I can truthfully say that from October, 1882, until February, 1883, that spirit followed me day and night telling me that I was unworthy to be an Apostle of the Church, and that I ought to resign. When I would testify of my knowledge that Jesus is the Christ, the Son of the Living God, the Redeemer of mankind, it seemed as though a voice would say to me: 'You lie! You lie! You have never seen Him.'

"While on the Navajo Indian reservation . . . on horseback . . . riding along with Lot Smith at the rear of that procession, suddenly the road veered to the left almost straight, but there was a well-beaten path leading ahead. . . .

"I said, 'Lot, is there any danger from Indians here?'

"'None at all.'

"'I want to be all alone. Go ahead and follow the crowd.' . . .

"As I was riding along to meet them on the other side I seemed to see, and I seemed to hear, what to me is one of the most real things in all my life. I seemed to see a council of heaven. I seemed to hear the words that were spoken. I listened to the discussion with a great deal of interest. The First Presidency and the Council of the Twelve Apostles had not been able to agree on two men to fill the vacancies in the Quorum of the Twelve. There had been a vacancy of one for two years, and a vacancy of two for one year, and the Conferences had adjourned without the vacancies being filled. In this Council the Savior was present, my father was there, and the Prophet Joseph Smith was there. They discussed the question that a mistake had been made in not filling those two vacancies and that in all probability it would be another six months before the Quorum would be completed; and they discussed as to whom they wanted to occupy those positions, and decided that the way to remedy the mistake that had been made in not filling these vacancies was to send a revelation. It was given to me that the Prophet Joseph Smith and my father mentioned me and requested that I be called to that position. I sat there and wept for joy. It was given to me that I had done nothing to entitle me to that exalted position, except that I had lived a clean, sweet life. It was given to me that because of my father having practically sacrificed his life in what was known as the great Reformation, so to speak, of the people in early days, having been practically a martyr, that the Prophet Joseph and my father desired me to have that position, and it was because of their faithful labors that I was called, and not because of anything I had done of myself or any great thing that I had accomplished. It was also given to me that that was all these men, the Prophet and my father, could do for me; from that day it depended upon me and upon me alone as to whether I made a success of my life or a failure."

The seventh president of the Church, Heber J. Grant served as an apostle for thirty-six years before succeeding Joseph F. Smith as prophet, seer, and revelator. Heber never knew the father he had pictured as he was riding the trail alone because forty-year-old Jedediah M. Grant, apostle and counselor to Brigham Young, died of "lung disease" on 1 December 1856, nine days after his son Heber was born.

Heber's mother, Rachel Ivins Grant, declined offers of financial help and moved from the spacious Grant home to a "widow's cabin." She supported herself and her son by sewing and taking in boarders. As a boy, Heber often sat on the floor pumping the sewing machine treadle to help his mother.

Hard work became Heber's trademark. He educated himself and joined the "Wasatch Literary Association," a group that met every Wednesday evening for debates, readings, lectures, and musical productions. (Other members included future Quorum of the Twelve president Rudger Clawson, future First Council of Seventy member Rulon S. Wells, and future governor of Utah Heber M. Wells.) Heber also sold books, taught himself excellent penmanship, represented a Chicago grocery house, and founded his own insurance agency.

Marrying at age twenty and called as Tooele Stake president three years later, Heber seemed to be thriving. Within a short time, however, his wife fell ill, his insurance business declined, and his Ogden vinegar factory burned down. Under these mounting pressures, twenty-four-year-old Heber saw his own health rapidly decline, and he suffered a nervous collapse. These circumstances no doubt led to Heber's sense of inadequacy when, less than a year later, John Taylor announced a revelation calling Heber as an apostle. But the profound spiritual insights he experienced while riding the Navajo Indian reservation changed all of that.

"It was given to me, as I say," he wrote, "that it now depended upon me.

"No man could have been more unhappy than I was from October, 1882, until February, 1883, but from that day I have never been bothered, night or day, with the idea that I was not worthy to stand as an Apostle. . . ."

President Grant continued, "I have been happy during the twenty-two years that it has fallen to my lot to stand at the head of this Church. I have felt the inspiration of the living God directing me in my labors. From the day that I chose a comparative stranger to be one of the Apostles, instead of my lifelong and dearest living friend, I have known as I know that I live, that I am entitled to the light and the inspiration and the guidance of God in directing His work here upon this earth; and I know, as I know that I live, that it is God's work, and that Jesus Christ is the Son of the Living God, the Redeemer of the world and that He came to this earth with a divine mission to die upon the cross as the Redeemer of mankind, atoning for the sins of the world.

". . . I have had joy in lifting my voice in England, Ireland, Scotland and Wales, Belgium, Holland, Switzerland, Germany, France, Italy, Norway, Sweden, Denmark, and Czechoslovakia, in the Hawaiian Islands and far-off Japan, in Canada on the north and Mexico on the south, in nearly every State of the Union, proclaiming my absolute knowledge that God lives, that Jesus is the Christ, the Son of the living God, the Redeemer of the world, and that I know that Joseph Smith was a prophet of the true and the Living God, and that the men who have succeeded him in presiding over this Church are the men God desired to stand in that position.

". . . I love the Gospel of Jesus Christ as I love nothing else in this world."

THREE GENERATIONS OF
APOSTLE MISSIONARIES

A father, son, and grandson were all members of the Quorum of the Twelve and all tireless missionaries. The father, an associate of Joseph Smith and other early Church leaders, was baptized at age seventeen and left home to join his younger brother in Missouri. When he reached Missouri, he heard of the massacre at Haun's Mill, and when he arrived at the actual site of the attack he found that his brother had been among those killed by the mob. Despite this tragedy, losing another brother as the result of the long march of the Mormon Battalion, and the deaths of two of his children on the journey from Nauvoo to Winter Quarters, he devoted himself to the work.

Ordained an apostle in 1849, he served four missions to Great Britain, three of them as mission president, and helped more than 30,000 Saints immigrate to Zion. During one of these missions, in 1851, he compiled several of his favorite documents into a tract and called it the Pearl of Great Price. In 1880, it was accepted at a general conference as one of the standard works. The last fifteen months of his life, the father served as president of the Quorum of the Twelve.

The son was born in 1861, when his father was thirty-nine. He was called to a stake presidency at the age of twenty-nine and ordained a patriarch three years later. He served faithfully and was known for his gentle manner and sense of honor. In 1906, he experienced a powerful dream of the Savior. He later recalled:

". . . more than 40 years ago I had a dream which I am sure was from the Lord. In this dream I was in the presence of my Savior as He stood in mid-air. He spoke no word to me, but my love for Him was such that I have not words to explain. I know no mortal man can love the Lord as I experienced that love for the Savior unless God reveals it to him. I would have remained in his presence, but there was a power drawing me away from him.

"As a result of that dream, I had this feeling that no matter what might be required at my hands, what the Gospel might entail unto me, I would do what I should be asked to do even to the laying down of my life."

Shortly after this dream—and six years after his father had died—the son was called to the Twelve. He was ordained an apostle the same day as Orson F. Whitney and David O. McKay. He served in the Quorum for forty-four years, including five years as president. From 1916 to 1919, during the trying years of World War I, he served as president of the European Mission.

The grandson was born in 1886, when his father was twenty-four and his grandfather was sixty-four. He was called on a mission from 1905 to 1908, and in 1913 returned to the same area as mission president, at the age of twenty-seven. As mission president, he had a unique ability to get close to the missionaries and earn their trust. "He seemed to know our thoughts," one of them wrote, "and he had feelings of love and compassion for us in our great weakness. I loved and admired the president and felt understood by him as I had never felt understood by mortal man. His will was my pleasure, and with joy I gave my best effort to the work, taking him as my hero."

At age sixty-six, the grandson was called to the Quorum of the Twelve, a year and a half after his father had died. Right after a session of conference, with no forewarning, he was asked to meet with President McKay, who told him he had been called to fill the vacancy occasioned by the death of Elder Joseph F. Merrill. "I wept and the President wept, and we hugged each other, and then we went over to the afternoon meeting," he recalled.

Franklin D. Richards, George F. Richards, and LeGrand Richards left a lasting legacy of missionary work. When LeGrand Richards died in 1983, the three men had served a combined (and incredible) 124 years of the 148-year existence of the Quorum of the Twelve. (Other three-generation apostles were Hyrum, Joseph F., and brothers Hyrum Mack and Joseph Fielding Smith; George A., John Henry, and George Albert Smith; and Amasa, Francis M., and Richard R. Lyman.)

This tradition of proclaiming the gospel culminated with the publication of LeGrand Richards's book *A Marvelous Work and a Wonder* in 1950. During the 1930s he had produced a pamphlet outlining the fundamental doctrines of the Church called "The Message of Mormonism." Over the next ten years he received continual requests to expand the pamphlet into a book. And so, during the 1940s, though he was extremely busy as presiding bishop of the Church, he began writing the book. As he traveled to conferences, he wrote on the train or at any other opportunity. Of one trip he said, "I sat in the motel writing until my eyes were so tired that I was sick to my stomach."

Members and investigators alike responded to the book with unusual enthusiasm, buying close to two million copies over the next thirty years. Elder Richards declined any royalties.

"I've watched the book go through printing after printing," said President Thomas S. Monson, sales manager of Deseret News Press at the time. " . . . [The book] is mass-produced like no other LDS book except the Book of Mormon. It is a missionary in print.

"We wore out nickel and chromium-surfaced electrotype plates of LeGrand's book because it had to be reprinted so many times on such long runs. It is a phenomenon!"

REMEMBERING
JOSEPH'S FAMILY

In May of 1871, a quarter of a century after the Saints left Nauvoo, the following letter was sent to a relative of Joseph Smith's who had remained in Illinois and was then living in the town of Fountain Green:

"Dear Sister,

"Your letter of the 29th. April was duly received. I send you Two hundred (200) dollars at your request and I sincerely trust it will prove the blessing you anticipate.

"Elder Warren N. Dusenbury, who has been instructed to bear it to you, will give you all the news, much of which will doubtless prove interesting: you will find him a gentleman worthy of your consideration, and he is well acquainted with the leaders of the Church, and many others, possibly with whom you are acquainted, I think you will appreciate his society. He will convey to you our best regards. The memory of our beloved Prophet is deeply cherished in the hearts of the Saints, and for his sake, his relations and members of his family, notwithstanding differences of opinion are kindly regarded and would be welcomed among us and received with open arms, were they willing to adhere to the principles taught by the Prophet and become one with those who are striving night and day with all their hearts to carry out those principles he held so sacred and taught his brethren.

"May peace be with you and the blessings of Heaven attend you all the remnant of your days upon the earth, and a happy hereafter be your lot in eternity.

"Your Bro. in the Gospel"

Katharine Smith Salisbury, younger sister of Joseph Smith, had been a widow for almost twenty years when she wrote Brigham Young for help in buying a house. Brigham sent additional funds beyond the initial $200, and Katharine responded with notes thanking "Brother Brigham" and praying for the blessing of heaven to be with "all the Church." When her cousin apostle George A. Smith personally stopped to help her, she expressed "unbounded" gratitude and reflected that "it seemed like old times to meet with the Servant of the Lord."

Born in 1813, Katharine was eight years younger than Joseph Smith and therefore fourteen years old when Joseph received the plates in 1827. She later wrote: "After [Joseph] had the vision, he went frequently to the hill, and upon returning would tell us, 'I have seen the records, also the brass plates and the sword of Laban with the breast plate and interpreters.' . . . We had supposed that when he should bring them home, the whole family would be allowed to see them, but he said it was forbidden of the Lord. . . . We had therefore to be content until they were translated and we could have the book to read. Many times when I have read its sacred pages, I have wept like a child, while the Spirit has borne witness with my spirit to its truth."

In 1885, Elder Victor E. Bean visited Katharine. As he said good-bye he asked if she would ever come to Utah to see relatives. "She began to sob and said, to have the elders call on her, traveling as we were, carried her mind back to early days when her brothers used to go in the same way to preach the gospel." She said further that while age and poverty prevented her from going west, she wished for future visits from LDS elders and "desired an interest in our prayers."

Katharine was the sole surviving member of Joseph Sr. and Lucy's family when she died at age eighty-six in 1900.

THE CANE
CREEK MASSACRE

In the autumn of 1809, three years after his famous exploration of the American West had ended, Meriwether Lewis rode through Tennessee on his way to the nation's capital. On a warm October evening he pulled his horse off a trail known as the Natchez Trace and stopped at Griner's Stand, an inn that offered food and lodging to travelers of the Trace. Within hours, Lewis died a mysterious death from two gunshot wounds. Some said they were self-inflicted, but others argued Lewis was murdered. Lewis's death was a source of endless controversy, and it was also an omen of future events. Ten or fifteen miles from where Lewis died, in an area known for its lush woods, wildlife, and waterfalls, four Church members would also die violent deaths.

Though early missionaries David W. Patten, Warren Parrish, and Wilford Woodruff had preached the gospel in several Tennessee counties in the late 1830s, missionary work there had stopped after the exodus west. It resumed in 1870 when Elder Hayden Church arrived, and five years later the Southern States Mission was organized, with headquarters in Tennessee.

In Lewis County, named after the famed explorer, several families accepted the gospel, but opposition arose against them. On the Sabbath morning of 10 August 1884, near a stream called Cane Creek (north of present-day Hohenwald, Tennessee), three missionaries—William S. Berry, Henry Thompson, and John H. Gibbs—prepared for Church services at the home of converts James and Rachel Condor. Fellow elder William H. Jones had lingered briefly at the home of a friend to read an issue of the *Deseret News*, and as he walked toward the Condor cabin, he was abducted by twelve or fourteen men dressed in Ku Klux Klan hoods and robes. They held Elder Jones hostage and demanded to know where the others were.

The mob crept toward the Condor home just as services were about to begin. When one of the mob grabbed James Condor, he yelled to his son, Martin, and his stepson, James Hudson, to get their guns. As Martin ran to the living room for his rifle, he and Elder Gibbs, still holding his Bible, were shot down by the mob. Several other shots rang out. A mobster aimed a gun at Elder Thompson, but Elder Berry pushed it aside, allowing Thompson to run out the back door into the woods. Seconds after saving Thompson's life, Berry himself was shot several times and fell dead.

Young Hudson had just retrieved his Kentucky rifle from the attic when two mobsters seized him at the doorway. He fought them off and shot Dave Hinson, the murderer of Elder Gibbs. Hinson died instantly. Enraged at his death, the mob screamed oaths of revenge and fired a volley of shots at Hudson and anyone else inside the house. Then they retrieved Hinson's body and fled. Inside the house, Hudson lay mortally wounded, and Mrs. Condor had suffered a gunshot to her hip that would leave her disabled for the rest of her life. In the chaos, Elder Jones had escaped and run to a neighboring town for help.

The mission president was across the state in Chattanooga, unaware of the tragedy. The next evening he worked on an article he was writing for the *Juvenile Instructor*. When he finished he put out the lamp, but, as he recalled, "To my astonishment there was no diminution of the light in the room. Every object was as vividly seen as before the lamp was extinguished. This of course was something of a mystery to me and instead of immediately retiring I walked about the room trying to account for the strange phenomenon. . . . I lay marveling at it for some hours, nearly through the night, in fact. But with the

breaking of day I fell into a restless sleep and when I awoke the sunshine was brightly slanting in the room from the east."

More than forty years later, when he spoke at the funeral of Elder
Gibbs's widow, the mission president said the inexplicable light had
been an effort from Elder Gibbs to communicate with him and prepare
him for the news of the murders.

After waking Tuesday morning, the mission president walked to
the hotel where he normally ate breakfast. "As I entered the foyer of
the Hotel all eyes seemed intent upon me but no one spoke. When the
morning paper was brought to me I was astonished to see in glaring
headlines an account of the Mormon elders being massacred on Cane
Creek in Lewis County. It was too horrible to believe. Neglecting
breakfast I returned to headquarters that I might ask in prayer if this
terrible thing were true. While on my knees in the office of the
Mission, engaged in prayer, the voice which so frequently spoke to me
in times of crisis, bade me return to the Hotel where I would receive a
message. At the Hotel I found a telegram from . . . the [mission] secretary, confirming the newspaper account of the killing of the elders and
the Condor boys."

The mission president purchased steel coffins to return the bodies
of Elder Gibbs and Elder Berry to Utah. The president later reported
that the Spirit prompted him, "You will go to secure those bodies and
all will be well with you. But *you* must go." He then traveled to
Columbia, Tennessee, thirty miles east of where the murders had
occurred, where he met the mission secretary and the other elders.
Their lives had been threatened, and the president moved them from
a boarding house into a hotel and, while they slept, wrote a full
account of the murders to Church authorities. The next morning the
mission president and secretary prayed about how to retrieve the bodies of the slain elders.

"I was at Shady Grove and was the first to get the information of the killing of Elders Gibb, Berry and the Condor boys, and of their burial," recalled the mission secretary, J. Golden Kimball. He added that he and the mission president "kneeled down and prayed, and we discussed the matter and were satisfied that we should secure the bodies. I said: " . . . let me go. They know you in that section. You have preached there. They will kill you. Let me go."

The twenty-seven-year-old mission president, B. H. Roberts, said, "No, I am the president of the mission. The Lord will take care of me."

Decades later, Elder Roberts reminisced: "Brother Kimball not only volunteered, but was insistent that he should go to recover the bodies of these two elders and thus spare me the danger. His offer was as generous as it was sincere. But, finally, I prevailed upon Brother Kimball that I should take the risk, pointing out that with that long, lean, greyhound figure of his, effective disguise would be impossible and that the danger from our enemies, bitter and enraged as they were, would be too great if he were to go."

Thirty-one-year-old Elder J. Golden Kimball, still weak from a bout with malaria, finally relented. He watched as President Roberts "disguised himself by shaving his beard and mustache, dressing in a suit of mismatched old clothing, wearing a slouched hat and rough cowhide boots, and rubbing soot grease from the smokehouse walls over his face. He was a hard-looking sight. No one recognized him, not even a young friend, Robert Coleman, whom he asked: 'Robert, I am going to [Cane Creek] with two teams to secure the bodies of the elders who have been murdered. Brothers Church and Harlow have consented to take one wagon. Will you go with me and drive the other wagon?' 'Why yes, Mr. Roberts, I'll go anywhere with you, Sir!' The youth was not a member of the Church. 'This direct answer, this symbol of trust and fidelity,' Roberts later wrote, 'shook me with emotion.'"

When the four men reached the graves, a crowd—including some of the mob—had gathered to watch. President Roberts spoke with a southern accent as he and his companions wrapped the bodies in clean sheets and placed them in the new coffins. When he saw Sister Condor, grieving from the death of her two sons and suffering from her own injury, he longed to reveal his identity and comfort her, but he had to remain silent.

The two elders, thirty-one-year-old John H. Gibbs of northern Utah, and forty-six-year-old William Shanks Berry of Kanarra, Utah, were thus returned home for their final rest. Elder Gibbs, a schoolteacher born in Wales, left a wife, Louisa Obray, and several children. ". . . He was naturally gifted, being fluent in speech, easy and pleasant in conversation . . . ," wrote President Roberts. "But to crown it all, he was an honorable man, ever prayerful and humble in spirit—a truly Christian man." Elder Berry, a native of Tennessee who had lived in Nauvoo as a boy, was survived by his elderly mother and a brother. Two of his other brothers had been killed by Indians in southern Utah in 1866. President Roberts said he "was somewhat slow of speech, but endowed to a remarkable degree with good, sound sense, and was of a mild and genial disposition."

Lifelong friends B. H. Roberts and J. Golden Kimball were named to the First Council of the Seventy in 1888 and 1892, respectively, and served together for four decades. "The first time I ever saw Elder Roberts," said Elder Kimball, "was either in Cincinnati or St. Louis. He had been chosen as president of the Southern States Mission to succeed John Morgan. I left for Chattanooga, Tennessee, with twenty-seven elders, assigned to the Southern States. There were all kinds of elders in the company; farmers, cowboys, few educated—a pretty hard looking crowd, and I was one of that kind. The elders preached, and

talked, and sang; and advertised loudly their calling as preachers. I
kept still for once in my life; I hardly opened my mouth. I saw a gentleman get on the train. I can visualize that man now. I didn't know
who he was. He knew we were a band of Mormon elders. The elders
soon commenced a discussion and argument with the stranger, and
before he got through they were in grave doubt about their message of
salvation. He gave them a training that they never forgot. That man
proved to be President B. H. Roberts."

After serving in the mission field for one year, Golden was called
to be secretary to President Roberts. "I talked with him," Golden said.
"He trusted me, and I never betrayed him. He confided in me, the only
time in his life, about his own affairs, his family, etc. We occupied one
room—used as office and sleeping quarters. We paid twenty-five dollars a month for rent and board. It was hotter than hades most of the
time. I was his secretary. He walked the floor and dictated (and I wrote
long-hand) volumes and stored away a fund of information."

When B. H. Roberts died in 1933 at age seventy-six, Elder Kimball
mourned his loss: "Eight members of the First Council have died since
I was ordained on October 8, 1892, and there isn't one of that number who was so close to me as Brigham H. Roberts. I never felt more
lonely or helpless, in a way, than I do now. Brother Roberts has been
my mentor; he has been my teacher; he has been my chronicler. I was
relieved of reading the great histories; I didn't have to read a whole
library searching for information. What did I have to do? When anything troubled me about the history of the Church or scripture, I went
to Brother Roberts. He had the most wonderful mind and memory of
any human being I have ever known, right up to the very last. A great
light has gone out in my life. I will soon follow."

THE FIRST
SISTER MISSIONARIES

A t a street meeting in northwestern England in 1898, an announcement was made that "real live Mormon women" would speak the next day. The news spread through the town of Oldham. Orson F. Whitney recorded what happened the next day:

"The hall was crowded, and their remarks were listened to with rapt attention. The novel spectacle of two young and innocent girls— whose appearance alone betokened modesty and virtue, as their utterances showed intelligence and sincerity—declaring in words of soberness that Mormonism was divine, that it had made them what they were, and had sent them forth to bear witness of its truth, was a revelation to many."

The two young women who spoke were the first single sisters set apart as missionaries. They had arrived with a group of elders in Liverpool, England, on 22 April 1898. Like the elders, the sisters spoke at street meetings and tracted. Though they were initially greeted with curiosity, attitudes usually changed. As one of the sisters wrote, "But when I go with second tracts they will then know that I am Mormon and I do not expect all kind treatment. I like my work very much and I feel as if I don't care how long I am required to labor as an ambassador for Christ, but I do not always feel the same."

Active opposition was not uncommon. One day when they were going house to house, a vocal woman followed them, discouraging her neighbors from listening to the gospel message. One person's journal entry summed up, "Attended regular meeting in the evening. Much disturbance, had to call a policeman to clear the hall."

Amanda Inez Knight and Lucy Jane Brimhall were friends from Provo, Utah, who had been planning a trip to Europe when they were called on missions. Inez, the daughter of influential businessman Jesse Knight and his wife Amanda McEwan, was twenty-two and had been active in researching her family history. "Jennie" Brimhall, twenty-three, was the daughter of future Brigham Young Academy president George Brimhall and his wife Alsina Wilkins and had worked as a schoolteacher.

The two served as companions until November of 1898, when concerns over Sister Brimhall's health brought about her release. She returned to the United States with a group of missionaries that included Sister Knight's brother William Knight. William and Jennie were married a few months later and helped found the town of Raymond, Alberta, Canada. After returning to the United States, Jennie served as a counselor to Clarissa S. Williams in the general Relief Society presidency.

Liza Chipman was Inez's new companion, and the two faced increasing persecution. One evening a group called the Anti-Mormon League taunted the sisters and threw rocks and trash at them, harassing them all the way to a police station. "Arriving at the station, we were at once hurried into a back room, and after waiting there about an hour (in which time some tears were shed and a Gospel conversation held) the chief of police took us out of the rear entrance and saw us safely home."

Sister Knight labored in England until May 1900. In 1902 she married Robert Eugene Allen, and they had five sons. She served on the Relief Society General Board and was active in the Red Cross and the Democratic party.

A LETTER FROM A
FUTURE CHURCH PRESIDENT

After Charles E. Callis and his wife, Grace, had served in the mission field for almost three decades, Brother Callis was called to serve in the Quorum of the Twelve. On 10 October 1933, two days before Charles was ordained an apostle, Grace, who was still at the mission home in Atlanta, Georgia, received the following letter from an apostle and future Church president:

"[My wife] and I have been talking about you and concluded that the proper thing at this time was for me to write a letter for both of us.

"We congratulate you whole-heartedly on the honor that has come to you and your dear husband. It has come to both of you for he could never have accomplished what he has without your faithful and devoted assistance."

The apostle went on to say that it had been his desire to see Samuel O. Bennion and Brother Callis both among the General Authorities of the Church. ". . . that has now come to pass. I hope and believe they will both be very happy in the work."

The apostle reported that his wife was still confined at home, "but I feel sure she is making a little gain. She will make you most welcome when you come back to Salt Lake and we are both glad that we will be near enough to have your companionship and that of your dear husband more frequently than in the past."

Such a letter was characteristic of the friendliness and gentle nature of George Albert Smith. As Richard L. Evans said of him in the October 1945 general conference, "He is considerate and loving and kindly under all circumstances, and on all occasions." Elder Smith helped Brother Callis get settled in his new location and reported to Grace that her husband was occupying a "very comfortable delightful" office that Elder Smith himself had previously used.

George Albert Smith had married Lucy Emily Woodruff, a granddaughter of Wilford Woodruff, in 1892. They served together in the Southern States Mission under President J. Golden Kimball, and, after George's call to the apostleship, in the British Mission. Lucy was in ill health when George wrote the above letter, and she died four years later at age sixty-eight.

Elder Callis served as an apostle for more than fourteen years. His wife, Grace, passed away in the fall of 1946, and he never recovered from her loss. He was visiting a stake conference in the South, where he and Grace had served with such devotion, when he died in January of 1947.

George Albert Smith had been president of the Church for almost two years when Elder Callis died. Throughout his service as Church president, he continued to make friends in and out of the Church. When he died in 1951, the following telegram sent to his children typified the emotions of many:

> Deeply distressed over your bereavement. I know the whole State of Utah has suffered a grievous loss. Your father carried an historic burden with foresight and courage. I had looked forward eagerly to his counsel and friendship. Please know I am thinking of you and keeping you in my prayers.
>
> Richard S. Watson
> Episcopal Bishop Elect of Utah

"WHEN I WAS YOUNG": LIFE-CHANGING MOMENTS

THE OLD
PROPHET MASON

Writing his autobiography, a man told how a remarkable prophecy was fulfilled:

"I spent the first years of my life under the influence of . . . the 'Blue Laws.' . . .

"No man, boy or child of any age was permitted to play or do any work from sunset Saturday night until Sunday night. After sunset on Sunday evening, men might work, and boys might jump, shout and play as much as they pleased.

"Our parents were very strict with us on Saturday night, and all day Sunday we had to sit very still and say over the Presbyterian catechism and some passages in the Bible.

"The people . . . in those days thought it wicked to believe in any religion, or belong to any church, except the Presbyterian. They did not believe in having any prophets, apostles, or revelations, as they had in the days of Jesus, and as we now have in the Church of Jesus Christ of Latter-day Saints.

"There was an aged man . . . , however, by the name of Robert Mason, who did not believe like the rest of the people. He believed it was necessary to have prophets, apostles, dreams, visions and revelations in the church of Christ, the same as they had who lived in ancient days; and he believed the Lord would raise up a people and a church, in the last days, with prophets, apostles, and all the gifts, powers and blessings, which it ever contained in any age of the world.

"The people called this man, the Old Prophet Mason.

"He frequently came to my father's house when I was a boy, and taught me and my brothers those principles; and I believed him.

"This prophet prayed a great deal, and he had dreams and visions and the Lord showed him many things, by visions, which were to come to pass in the last days.

"I will here relate one vision, which he related to me. The last time I ever saw him, he said: 'I was laboring in my field at mid-day when I was enwrapped in a vision. I was placed in the midst of a vast forest of fruit trees: I was very hungry, and walked a long way through the orchard, searching for fruit to eat; but I could not find any in the whole orchard, and I wept because I could find no fruit. While I stood gazing at the orchard, and wondering why there was no fruit, the trees began to fall to the ground upon every side of me, until there was not one tree standing in the whole orchard; and while I was marveling at the scene, I saw young sprouts start up from the roots of the trees which had fallen, and they opened into young, thrifty trees before my eyes. They budded, blossomed, and bore fruit until the trees were loaded with the finest fruit I ever beheld, and I rejoiced to see so much fine fruit. I stepped up to a tree and picked my hands full of fruit, and marveled at its beauty, and as I was about to taste of it the vision closed, and I found myself in the field in the same place I was at the commencement of the vision.

"'I then knelt upon the ground, and prayed unto the Lord, and asked Him, in the name of Jesus Christ, to show me the meaning of the vision. The Lord said unto me: "This is the interpretation of the vision: the great trees of the forest represented the generation of men in which you live. There is no church of Christ, or kingdom of God upon the earth in your generation. There is no fruit of the church of Christ upon the earth. There is no man ordained of God to administer in any of the ordinances of the gospel of salvation upon the earth in this day and generation. But, in the next generation, I the Lord will set up my kingdom and my church upon the earth, and the fruits of the kingdom and church of Christ, such as have followed the prophets, apostles and saints in every dispensation, shall again be found in all their fullness upon the earth. You will live to see the day, and handle the fruit; but will never partake of it in the flesh.'"

"When the old prophet had finished relating the vision and interpretation, he said to me, calling me by my Christian name: 'I shall never partake of this fruit in the flesh; but you will, and you will become a conspicuous actor in that kingdom.' He then turned and left me. These were the last words he ever spoke to me upon the earth.

"This was a very striking circumstance, as I had spent many hours and days, during twenty years, with this old Father Mason, and he had never named this vision to me before. But at the beginning of this last conversation he told me that he felt impelled by the Spirit of the Lord to relate it to me.

"He had the vision about the year 1800, and he related it to me in 1830—the same spring that the Church was organized.

"This vision, with his other teachings to me, made a great impression upon my mind, and I prayed a great deal to the Lord to lead me by His Spirit, and prepare me for His church when it did come.

". . . in the winter of 1833, I saw, for the first time in my life, an Elder of the Church of Jesus Christ of Latter-day Saints. He preached in a schoolhouse near where I lived. I attended the meeting, and the Spirit of the Lord bore record to me that what I heard was true . . . and next day I, with my eldest brother, went down into the water and was baptized. We were the first two baptized in Oswego County, New York."

The young friend of the prophet Mason left a meticulous record of his life—more than 7,000 pages of diaries that span the years from 1833 to his death in 1898. Born in Connecticut in 1807, Wilford Woodruff searched for the kind of Church prophesied by Robert Mason and joined with a group of like-minded individuals to study the scriptures. By 1833, Wilford and his brother Azmon had bought a farm in Richland, New York, a town near Lake Ontario. In December of that year, Latter-day Saint missionaries Zera Pulsipher and Elijah Cheney began preaching the gospel in Richland. They taught with power and gave priesthood blessings. Impressed by their message, Azmon and Wilford were baptized on 31 December 1833. Wilford was twenty-six years old.

"When I was baptized," he wrote, "I thought of what the old prophet had said to me."

Within months, Wilford received a call from Parley P. Pratt to travel to Kirtland, Ohio, and join Joseph Smith and more than two hundred others in marching to Missouri to relieve the persecuted Saints there. This relief expedition became known as Zion's Camp. Wilford quickly put his financial affairs in order and left for Ohio. He first met Joseph and Hyrum Smith when they were shooting at targets with a pair of pistols. Joseph invited Wilford to stay with him. Wilford met Brigham Young and Heber C. Kimball the next day and soon heard sermons by Orson Pratt, Sidney Rigdon, and Orson Hyde. Wilford remarked that "there was more light made manifest at that meeting respecting the gospel and Kingdom of God than I had ever received from the whole Sectarian world."

A group of 207 men, 11 women, and 11 children left Kirtland early in May of 1834. After averaging thirty-five miles a day, Zion's Camp neared Independence, Missouri, by 19 June. They were spared a likely battle with a well-armed group of 300 men at Fishing River when a ferocious hailstorm descended on the Missourians, which Wilford called "the mandated vengeance . . . gone forth from the God of Battles to protect his servants from the Destruction of their enemies." The group also suffered many hardships, including an outbreak of cholera that claimed thirteen lives. Although Zion's Camp accomplished few of its secular objectives, it was an invaluable proving ground for future leaders of the Church. Wilford wrote that the expedition was "a great school for us to be led by a Prophet of God a thousand miles, through cities, towns, villages, and through the wilderness." Nine of the original apostles were members of Zion's Camp.

"In the spring of 1834, I went to Kirtland, saw the Prophet Joseph Smith, and went with him, and with more than two hundred others in Zion's Camp, up to Missouri," wrote Wilford. "When I arrived, at my journey's end, I took the first opportunity and wrote a long letter to Father Mason, and told him I had found the church of Christ that he had told me about. I told him about its organization and the coming forth of the Book of Mormon; that the Church had Prophets, Apostles, and all the gifts and blessings in it, and that the true fruit of the kingdom and church of Christ were manifest among the Saints as the Lord had shown him in the vision. He received my letter and read it over many times, and handled it as he had handled the fruit in the vision; but he was very aged, and soon died. He did not live to see any Elder to administer the ordinances of the gospel unto him.

"The first opportunity I had, after the doctrine of baptism for the dead was revealed, I went forth and was baptized for him. He was a good man and a true prophet, for his prophecies have been fulfilled."

"A Leader and an Interpreter"

In October of 1914, the same year World War I erupted in Europe, a young elder boarded a train in Salt Lake City to depart for the mission field. "A great many of my friends were at the depot to bid me goodbye and wish me success," he wrote in his journal. "At 4:15 P.M. our train pulled out and we were on our way to San Francisco."

After a month's journey, the elder arrived in the mission field. A few days later, he wrote, "We had a Thanksgiving dinner at headquarters and it was certainly a treat." The next morning he arrived in a town where he labored for several months. His first letter from home did not reach him until 10 December, more than six weeks after he started his mission. He wrote that he "was certainly glad to get it."

His missionary journal noted difficulties common to many missionaries: he was sick for two days with a stomach ailment; he was honored to perform his first baptism; he did his laundry and dropped off his shoes to get them mended; he was delighted to get a fruitcake from home; he was running out of money and anxious to get a money draft from home.

"The fleas bothered me so much that I was unable to sleep," he wrote one day. But the young elder showed a hearty optimism: "I call them my best companions because they stick to me so close." He soon began rubbing flea powder over his entire body and sprinkling it liberally on his covers before going to bed. "I trust that this will stupify them."

Years later, this elder wrote of how he was strengthened by the prayers of his family: "For eight months I was very sick," he later wrote.

"I had boils, sunstroke, tapeworms, was kicked in the abdomen by a horse, and it was just one thing after another. I used to wake up in the morning, and I would say to myself, 'Well, all of them at home, my father, mother, and brothers and sisters are down on their knees offering up their prayers in my behalf.' And when the dusk would come and night would fall, I would know that over 8,000 miles away my family were on their knees offering up their prayers, and that in their prayers my name was being mentioned. That meant something to me."

Within two months of his arrival in the mission field, the young elder was without a companion. He battled homesickness by studying the native language and by visiting friends and investigators. His journal entry for 8 February 1915 reads: "This is a very lonely place and I am afraid that I would be inclined to be homesick if I didn't have my books to study. . . . After studying several hours I took a walk up the road to another . . . home. Here I made some new friends and had a little religious conversation."

Shortly before his death, this man wrote that his mission experiences "have since been an anchor to my faith. It was there that I learned that there is saintliness in sinners; that sinners sometimes manifest greater love than some so-called Saints. It was there that I descended below all things and rose to the greatest heights of loving the weakest of the weak. . . . It was there that I learned the value of patience, long suffering, kindliness, forgiveness and the other virtues that are so necessary in the regeneration of the human soul. No greater respect have I ever received as a bearer of the priesthood than I did from [them], both members and non-members alike. When I was there as a mere boy they would come all hours of the night and day for confession, and for counsel and for administration. 'And a little child shall lead them.' They taught me the significance of this scripture."

In a patriarchal blessing he received when he was six years old, Matthew Cowley was promised: "Thou shalt become an ambassador of Christ to the uttermost bounds of the earth. . . . You shall be sent as a delegate to the ten tribes and will become a leader and an interpreter in the midst of that people, and because of the power of God that shall be with you, and the blessings of the Almighty, you shall be greatly beloved by that people."

When he was seventeen, young Matthew was called on a mission to the Hawaiian Islands. "I wanted to go there, and I was called to go there," he wrote. "One evening, President Anthon Lund, Counselor to President Smith, who was our next-door neighbor, came in to see me. . . . He looked at me and smiled and he said to me, ' . . . I was having dinner tonight and the Spirit told me you should go to New Zealand. I don't know why. That's the way I feel. If it is all right with you, I will tell President Smith in the morning, and you will be changed to New Zealand instead of the Hawaiian Islands.'"

And it was in New Zealand where the patriarch's prophecies saw profound fulfillment: Matthew clearly felt at ease with the Maori people and took an interest in their culture and language, becoming so fluent that he became "a leader and an interpreter" in a quite unexpected way: "After I had been in New Zealand for three years, I felt I should go home. My brothers were getting into the army. I wanted to be patriotic, but a cablegram came from the First Presidency [Joseph F. Smith and counselors Anthon H. Lund and Charles W. Penrose at that time]. It said, 'Keep Brother Cowley out there to translate the Doctrine and Covenants and Pearl of Great Price into the Maori language."

Elder Cowley stayed an additional two years. "I am the war missionary of New Zealand," he wrote. "I went in 1914, and they started the war. I went back in 1938 [as mission president], and they started another one. I was there during the whole period of both of those wars."

A few days after he arrived for his first mission, Elder Cowley wrote of the memorable, loving way Maoris greet visitors: "The visitors stand a few yards away from the people until all the [Maori] people have said a few words to greet them and make them welcome. Then the visitors go around and 'Hongi' (rub noses) with everyone. All this time the people are crying. After this is over they begin to sing and dance."

He later wrote, "I used to rub noses with them. That's what makes my nose turned down on the end there. It used to be straight. It's a wonderful custom."

Interestingly, when apostle David O. McKay and Hugh J. Cannon visited New Zealand in 1921, someone suggested that the "hongi" might not be appropriate. "What?" asked Elder McKay, who overheard the conversation. "We desire to be greeted in the traditional fashion."

Called as an apostle shortly after World War II ended, Elder Cowley again returned to his beloved New Zealand as the presiding General Authority over the entire Pacific region. Not long before his death at age fifty-three from a heart attack, he reflected on his first mission:

"It was there I came to know that poverty may be priceless as a source of genuine happiness. I have never seen a happier nor more fun-loving folk than were they. And they still are. Their happiness was punctuated with inter-family feuds, quarrels, but the grudges were soon forgotten. They would 'cuss' each other one minute and sing together the next. There amidst fleas and filth, I loved and was loved."

HEARTBREAK
IN NAUVOO

Afourteen-year-old young woman from Massachusetts joined the Church in 1842. One year later, in an arranged marriage, she wed James H. Harris, only two months her senior. He was the son of the New Salem, Massachusetts, branch president. The couple soon moved with James's parents to Nauvoo. Within months of their arrival, however, the young woman, still only sixteen, endured a series of tragedies. She, along with the entire community, mourned when Joseph and Hyrum were killed at Carthage Jail in June of 1844. Not long after that, James's parents left the Church and left Nauvoo as well. The young woman gave birth to a son, Eugene Henri Harris, but he died shortly after birth. Finally, James departed Nauvoo on a steamboat to look for work in New Orleans. The young woman waited patiently and tried not to lose hope, even when it appeared more and more likely that she had been abandoned.

On 20 February 1845, she confided to her diary: "When will sorrow leave my bosom? All my days have I experienced it; oppression has been my lot. When, O when shall I escape the bondage? Is not my life a romance—indeed it is a novel strange and marvellous. Here am I brought to this great city by one to whom I ever expected to look for protection and [am] left dependent on the mercy and friendship of strangers."

Three days later she wrote, "Last night there came a steamboat up the river. O how my youthful heart fluttered with hope with anxiety— my limbs were affected to that degree I was obliged to lay aside my work. I rely upon the promises he has made me and not all that has yet been said can shake my confidence in the only man I ever loved. . . . I watched the boat; I looked out at the door; I walked a few steps out of the yard; I saw a person approaching. My heart beat with fond anticipation. It walked like James. I came nearer and just as I was about to speak his name, he spoke and I found I was deceived by the darkness. Last night I dreamed he came home. O, that it were reality. Heavenly Father, again bring us together. . . . Boats are coming; two have past today, and where is James? Can he have forgot all his promises, all his vows? No, never, they must sting him to the very soul, and I pray God that they may and that remorse of conscience will bring him back to the path of duty."

Though she received no letters from James, the young wife apparently learned that he had gone to sea. On 24 March, she wrote: "O God, I bless thee that in thy mercy thou hast this day permitted me to hear news from a distant shore and that thou art kind and tender, O God forgive my unbelief and save him the wave, give him dreams and visions of the night that he may know thy will, O Lord, and do it and grant that he may return to me and not forget his first love."

In June of 1845, in the final entry of her Nauvoo diary, she wrote: "Again have my friends in a distant country, at the home of my childhood, remembered me and him whom I love. They know not he is far away on the stormy ocean, perhaps sleeping in the bottom of the sea and perhaps tossed on his vessel by the furious winds that blow across the sea. This, though, is almost too much for human nature to bear—my heart aches, my brain is dizzy at the idea. It brings the past before me in all its various lights and shades with all its labyrinths, and in some places I see happiness pictured in its most vivid colors . . . and in others I see dark places where I could hardly distinguish the Hand of Providence."

Years later, she learned that James had been killed in a sailing accident in the Indian Ocean.

As these diary entries illustrate, Emmeline B. Wells was an educated woman who found her voice as a writer at a young age. She became a prominent Latter-day Saint essayist and poet and edited the *Woman's Exponent* for thirty-seven years.

In February of 1845, the month she turned seventeen, Emmeline married Newel K. Whitney, who turned fifty the same month. Newel, who had been called as the first bishop in Kirtland, Ohio, was sustained as the first bishop of the Church in October of 1844. Emmeline and Newel crossed the plains in 1848 and arrived in the Salt Lake Valley in October. Less than a month later, Emmeline gave birth to a daughter, Modelena. A second daughter, Melvina, was born in August of 1850. Both daughters lived to maturity.

Just a few weeks later, fifty-five-year-old Newel began complaining of a severe pain in his left side. It was diagnosed as bilious pleurisy. His condition rapidly deteriorated, and on Monday, 23 September 1850, Brigham Young, Heber C. Kimball, and others gathered at the Whitney home on City Creek to prayerfully plead that Newel's life be spared. But Newel died later that day, and Emmeline, now only twenty-two, was left alone for the second time.

Two years later Emmeline married Newel's friend Daniel H. Wells. During much of this marriage, Emmeline suffered from the same loneliness she had already experienced. "O, if my husband could only love me even a little and not seem to be perfectly indifferent to any sensation of that kind," she wrote in her diary in 1874. "He cannot know the craving of my nature; he is surrounded with love on every side, and I am cast out. . . . O my poor aching heart. When shall it rest its burden? Only on the Lord. Every other avenue seems closed against me."

As the *Encyclopedia of Mormonism* summarizes: "Although three daughters were born to the union (two of them died in young adulthood), only in the later years of their marriage did Emmeline find the love and companionship that she had so long desired, but had found so elusive."

The name of Emmeline B. Wells is closely linked with one of the great welfare projects in the history of the Church—the Relief Society wheat storage program. "In late September of 1876, President Young sent for Mrs. Emmeline B. Wells to come to his office as he had something of importance he wanted to discuss with her. When she arrived he told her he wanted the women of Zion to gather and store grain against a time of need or famine, and that he desired her to lead out in the movement. He spoke of drought, crop failure, and the tolls often taken by grasshoppers, and emphasized the fact that the wheat would be held as a reserve and constant protection."

Over the next four decades, Sister Wells wrote and spoke on the need to store grain and considered the program one of the most important tasks of her life. Two examples of how the wheat relieved suffering came in 1906. After an earthquake devastated San Francisco, the Relief Society sent a train carload of flour to help the victims. Within months, the Relief Society sent another shipment of flour to offer relief from a famine that had struck China.

In 1918, when the United States government needed additional grain for military troops, the Relief Society offered to donate a large quantity of wheat, but government officials elected to purchase it for more than $412,000. Afterwards, President Woodrow Wilson and his wife made a visit to Salt Lake City. They visited ninety-year-old Relief Society President Emmeline B. Wells, bedridden at the time, to personally thank her for the wheat.

STUDYING WITH WORLD-RENOWNED SCHOLARS

Shortly after he married, a young Latter-day Saint student had the opportunity to attend one of the leading universities in the world—Goettingen in Germany. He later wrote:

"The great University, the second oldest in the German Empire, was famous. Illustrious men, makers of our modern day, had taught or studied there. It was a gathering place for students from many countries. In the advanced laboratory in which I worked, the ten students represented eight different nationalities. Americans had sought out the institution of learning for more than a hundred years. Marble plaques on the houses gave the names of men who had become famous, who had lived there. Bancroft and Longfellow were among the Americans so honored.

"Herr Geheimrath Doctor Professor Tollens, for whose wisdom I had crossed continents and an ocean, was a short, full bearded, pleasant faced man, who was equally at ease in German, French, or English. A skull cap covering his bald head, [was] often set at a rakish angle, when big things were happening in the laboratory. He moved quickly from place to place, usually muttering words of help in the native language of the student. His favorite pose was to hold a test tube against the light, looking intently at the contents, meanwhile shaking his head vigorously, whether in praise or condemnation no one knew, until the oracle spoke. But he knew his subject, and was an exquisite experimenter. The laboratory was filled with the spirit of discovery. Men grew under its influence. Soon all of us learned to love the kindly, helpful, 'Herr Geheimrath,' (Privy Councillor) a title which the government bestowed upon him soon after our arrival in Goettingen."

For his doctor's dissertation, the young student decided to research tragacanth, a gum obtained from Asian or East European plants and used in the arts and in pharmacy. He wanted to find out what kind of sugar or starch it contained. "Whatever it was, it had eluded former research. It finally yielded to the pursuit, after I had tried every method known to me. It was found unexpectedly to be a rare five carbon atom sugar with a group of one carbon and three hydrogen atoms (methyl group) attached."

The student later reflected that "the Ph.D. degree is only a badge or label. The real meaning of the doctor's degree is that . . . the recipient is now able to advance his special subject unaided by teachers." He had done exactly that in his studies, making significant discoveries through his own experiments. He next used a spectrograph, an instrument that allows scientists to determine the chemical composition of a given substance by analyzing its light spectrum. Since he had discovered that tragacanth was a "methyl pentosan," he attempted to learn whether methyl pentosans were widely distributed among plants. "I found the methyl pentosans to be of general occurrence in the plant kingdom. Nothing more in the field of research was needed for the thesis which I wrote and which was promptly accepted."

This student went on to publish widely and gain international acclaim in the area of soil chemistry. His academic career took a different turn when he was called to the Quorum of the Twelve, where he served with similar distinction. He properly summed up his lifelong efforts when he said, "I want to say to you frankly that I have nothing to recommend me except one thing—and thousands of men can say the same thing—I have done a day's work all the days of my life; and if that can be spoken of me, I shall be quite satisfied."

Born in Norway on 31 January 1872, John A. Widtsoe lost his father when he was six years old. His father, also named John, was a schoolmaster but died before achieving the education he desired. At the burial, young John placed a rose on his father's casket as a pledge to give his best to his education. "From my earliest youth education became my objective," he wrote. "There was a real relish for learning in my soul."

In 1884, John and his mother and brother crossed the Atlantic and settled in Cache County, Utah. John attended Brigham Young College in Logan and graduated in 1891. He was then accepted at Harvard and attended with a group of other young Latter-day Saint men. These LDS students saved money by renting a house together in Cambridge, Massachusetts. John's mother, Anne Gaarden Widtsoe, supported him by sewing and by mortgaging all of her property.

"At that time," he wrote, "I was having my religious battles. Was Mormonism what it pretended to be? Did Joseph Smith tell the truth? I read, listened, compared, thought, prayed. It was a real search for truth. Out of it in time came the certain knowledge that the restored [gospel] is true and that Joseph Smith was indeed a Prophet, and the restorer of the simple true gospel of Jesus Christ. There has never been any doubt about it since that time of deep study and prayer."

John took full advantage of his opportunities at Harvard and graduated *summa cum laude*. While there, he met a granddaughter of Brigham Young who was attending classes one summer, Leah Eudora Dunford, daughter of the prominent writer Susa Young Gates. Leah was an outstanding writer in her own right. John and Leah were married in June of 1898. Two months later, they left for Germany, "full of the zest of life, and open-eyed for new scenes and wider horizons," as John later said.

"On November 20, 1899, having come down from Berlin, where I was then studying, and having made the usual calls on my professors, in full evening dress attire (including the tall 'stovepipe hat'), I took my doctor's examination in the 'Aula' of the University. Sixteen or eighteen professors sat around the long table and asked questions, some of them inopportune, for two or three hours. After waiting half an hour in the adjoining waiting room, I was called back, and informed that I had passed the examination 'magna cum laude' (with high honors), and that the University was pleased to bestow upon me the degrees of master of arts and doctor of philosophy. A special certificate was also awarded me to use should I decide to teach or enter the chemical industry of Germany. I thanked the professors, notably Geheimrath Tollens, telegraphed my wife the good news, slept soundly that night, and lunched with friends at our old 'pension,' owned by the sisters von Keudell, arranged for the publication of my thesis, and hurried back to Berlin, glad that this milestone had been passed. . . . And I never forgot God's help for I had always placed my needs before him."

After John and Leah returned to the U.S., he directed the experimental station at Utah Agricultural College and published influential books on dry farming and irrigation. He became president of the college (now Utah State University) and later the University of Utah. In 1921, when he was forty-nine, John was called to the Quorum of the Twelve. He and Leah had seven children. Daughters Anna and Leah both lived long lives, but sons John and Mark and daughter Mary all died as infants, and son Marsel died when he was twenty-four. John and Leah found comfort by befriending young people, inviting some to live in their home.

"I Was Left to Wallow in My Blood"

Early in the nineteenth century, a mother and her eight children, including a five-year-old boy, a three-year-old daughter, and a baby boy, were forced to move from one state to another in the dead of winter. The children's maternal grandmother, who had lived with the family for some time, initially accompanied them as they traveled by sleigh, but she was injured when the sleigh overturned. Forced to stay behind with one of her sons, the eighty-four-year-old grandmother wept as she bid farewell to her daughter and grandchildren. "My dear child," she said to her daughter, "I have lived long—my days are nearly numbered—I must soon exchange the things of this world for those which pertain to another state of existence, where I hope to enjoy the society of the blessed; and now, as my last admonition, I beseech you to continue faithful in the service of God to the end of your days, that I may have the pleasure of embracing you in another and fairer world above."

The grandmother died two years later, and her premonition that she would not see her daughter and grandchildren again proved prophetic. One of the sons, who was about ten years old at the time, later told how his father, who had gone ahead of the rest of the family, hired a man by the name of Caleb Howard to help relocate the family.

The son, who was still recovering from a serious illness, related, "After [Howard] had started on the journey with my mother and family, he spent the money he had received of my father in drinking and gambling. We fell in with a family by the name of Gates who were traveling west, and Howard drove me from the wagon and made me travel in my weak state through the snow forty miles per day for several days, during which time I suffered the most excruciating weariness and pain, and all this that Mr. Howard might enjoy the society of two of Mr. Gates's daughters which he took on the wagon where I should have rode, and thus he continued to do day after day through the journey, and when my brothers remonstrated with Mr. Howard for his treatment to me, he would knock them down with the butt of his whip."

Then, one morning as the family was preparing for the day's journey, the oldest son ran into the inn where they had spent the night. "Mother," he cried, "Mr. Howard has thrown the goods out of the wagon, and is about starting off with the team." The mother stopped Howard by seizing the reins of the horses. She then called him inside the inn and spoke to him before a large group of fellow travelers:

"Gentlemen and ladies, please give your attention for a moment. Now, as sure as there is a God is heaven, that team, as well as the goods, belong to my husband, and this man intends to take them from me, or at least the team, leaving me with eight children, without the means of proceeding on my journey." Turning to Howard, she said, "Sir, I now forbid you touching the team, or driving it one step further. You can go about your own business; I have no use for you. I shall take charge of the team myself, and hereafter attend to my own affairs."

Howard did leave, but the ten-year-old son's trials were not over. He tried to board the last sleigh, "but when that came up I was knocked down by the driver, one of Gates's sons, and left to wallow in my blood until a stranger came along, picked me up, and carried me to the town. . . . Howard having spent all our funds, my mother was compelled to pay our landlords' bills . . . in bits of cloth, clothing, and so on, the last payment being made with the earrings taken from my sister's ears."

The mother who moved her family was Lucy Mack Smith. Her ten-year-old son was Joseph.

Late in 1816, after three years of successive crop failures, the Joseph Smith Sr. family left Norwich, Vermont, for Palmyra, New York—a journey of more than three hundred miles. The last of the three years before their departure was known throughout the area as the year without a summer. Due to ash in the atmosphere from the explosion of a volcano in the Pacific the previous year, the summer was cold, and a snowstorm hit central Vermont in June. As Lucy Mack Smith wrote, the cold summer "almost caused a famine. This was enough; my husband was now altogether decided upon going to New York. He came in, one day, in quite a thoughtful mood, and sat down; after meditating some time, he observed that, could he so arrange his affairs, he would be glad to start soon for New York."

As historian Richard L. Bushman has written, "The Smiths came closer to destitution from 1814 to 1816 than at any point in their lives. . . . By 1816, the Smiths had woven themselves into the web of debts and credits that substituted for money at that period." The family was in debt because of the crop failures and also because of medical expenses related to Joseph Jr.'s leg infection of a few years earlier. Fortunately, one of the doctors who cared for Joseph was Nathan Smith (no relation), who was one of the leading surgeons in New England. Nathan Smith had probably saved Joseph from losing his leg, but Joseph was nevertheless in bed or on crutches for three years after the ordeal. He was still recovering, and still using crutches, when the family decided to depart for what was then essentially the frontier.

Joseph Sr. called on his creditors and did his best to set his financial affairs in order before he went ahead to New York. The day he left, eighteen-year-old Alvin and sixteen-year-old Hyrum "followed their father with a heavy heart some distance." After he reached Palmyra, Joseph Sr. sent a letter requesting the rest of the family to come to New York. Just as Lucy and her children were starting, however, several creditors came forward demanding payment. They had apparently declined Joseph Sr.'s earlier attempts to settle, hoping to take advantage of Lucy right before she left. Although two Norwich residents offered to take Lucy's case to court, she decided to pay $150 so she could leave free of debt. This was a considerable sum for that time and left her with less than $80.

As noted, Lucy exhausted all of her funds on the journey. "I arrived in Palmyra with a small portion of my effects, my babes, and two cents in money but perfectly happy in the society of my family," she wrote. "The joy I felt in throwing myself and my children upon the care and affection of a tender husband and father doubly paid me for all I had suffered. The children surrounded their father, clinging to his neck and covering his face with tears and kisses that were heartily reciprocated by him."

Joseph Sr. may have chosen the Palmyra area for several reasons: his brothers had previously moved to northern New York; construction was about to begin on the Erie Canal, just north of Palmyra; and Vermont newspapers had advertised fertile land in New York. In any event, this unpretentious farming community was about to become the setting for marvelous and historic events. Just north of the town of Palmyra was a farm owned by Martin Harris, who would become one of the Three Witnesses. In the town of Palmyra itself was the Grandin Bookstore, where the Book of Mormon would be printed. The Smith home was south of Palmyra, and nearby were the woods where young Joseph would experience the First Vision. Also nearby was "a hill of considerable size, and the most elevated of any in the neighborhood," where Joseph would receive the plates.

An Accident-Prone Boy
Grows Up to Be an Apostle

When he was quite young, a boy silently approached his father, who was chopping wood. A back swing of the ax struck the boy in the head, sending him sprawling and bleeding. Gathering his son in his arms, the father immediately gave him a blessing, then rushed him for medical care. The boy believed he would be healed by the blessing, and he soon recovered.

Not long after, he was standing in the back of a wagon when the horses suddenly moved backward, throwing him out onto the ground. The wagon wheel immediately passed over his head. Before his father could pull him away, the team of horses moved forward, running over the boy's head a second time. Again, the frightened father blessed his son and sought medical aid; again, the boy recovered.

At eight years old, the boy was afflicted with a hip-bone disease. For nine months, he wore a cast that stretched from his foot to his hip and around his waist. He missed a year of school and was forced to hobble around on crutches. After he was somewhat mobile, he and his brothers were playing in a neighbor's yard when a ram charged them. The brothers escaped, but the boy in the cast could not move fast enough. He attempted to hold off the ram's repeated charges with his hands. Finally a neighbor grabbed the crutches lying on the ground and fought off the angry animal. The plaster cast saved the boy from serious injury.

The young man tells of another narrow escape:

"We sold a lot of hay to different people in the community. The Bowen boys came for a big load one day and I was the only one at the

Ranch, so . . . I loaded the hay for them, and they asked me to drive the team away from the stack so they could scrape up the loose hay. I got the lines mixed and pulled the team toward the stack instead of away from it, which tipped the load over, and I fell underneath. The wheel ran over my arm and broke it. I felt around to find my crutches and then managed to crawl out from under the load. My arm was bent at an awful angle, but I wouldn't let the doctor set it until my father returned from the Basin Pasture to give me a blessing."

That same day, the young man's brother had been given a diary for his twelfth birthday. "Both bones were broken above the wrist," he wrote. "We found Dr. F. M. Davis prepared to set the bones."

At age nineteen, as he was preparing to leave on his mission, the young man was again on crutches, his enlarged knee in a cast. Although he was advised to delay his mission, he requested a blessing from his father and left on time, with neither cast nor crutch.

This young man suffered other accidents and also survived a dangerously high fever for many days during a bout with scarlet fever. Through it all, he came out unscathed, except for a limp resulting from his hip problems. One leg was an inch and a half shorter than the other, causing him frequent pain. But this did not prevent him from dancing, leg-wrestling, and performing hard physical labor. Indeed, he said so little about the problem that one of his adult daughters later said, "Why, Daddy didn't limp."

Despite brushes with death when he was young, LeGrand Richards had a long, rich life before him. When he died in 1983 one month short of ninety-seven, he was older than any other apostle in this dispensation.

When he was sixteen, LeGrand left the family home in Tooele, Utah, to attend school and work in Salt Lake City. At Salt Lake Business College, he attended the lectures of J. Reuben Clark Jr. and was in the Sunday School class of James E. Talmage, both future apostles. In December of 1903, LeGrand and his brother Joel planned to return to Tooele for Christmas. LeGrand later related what happened:

"It snowed about a foot the night before we were to go home by train. We took our grips down to the depot, where Joel waited while I went up to about Eighth East [867 First Avenue] to get Grandmother, Nanny Longstroth Richards, who was going to Tooele with us.

"The streetcars were tied up and delayed because of the snow, and by the time I arrived at Grandmother's she had become anxious and had left for the station. When I got back to Main Street, I ran the remaining way to the Union Pacific Depot and arrived just in time to wave goodbye to the train carrying Joel and Grandmother.

"With no other way to reach home, I went to the Farrington Livery Stables, rented a saddle horse, and started out in that snow for the long, cold ride so that I could be home with my loved ones.

"When I reached the Point of the Mountain, about halfway home, I was mighty glad to see George with team and buggy to pick me up. He had no knowledge that I was coming, but he had said, 'I know LeGrand; he'll be here.' We tied the horse to the side and I rode with him in the buggy. When we arrived at our home, I got cleaned up and went to a dance that night. The next day I had a glorious Christmas with the folks."

In 1905, young LeGrand was called on a mission to the Southern States. His bishop, Oscar F. Hunter, was impressed, however, that LeGrand should serve in Europe. When Bishop Hunter communicated his feelings to the First Presidency, LeGrand's call was changed to Holland. (LeGrand's call to the Southern States Mission was in a way postponed rather than canceled: almost thirty years later, in 1934, he was called as president of that mission.)

LeGrand was determined to go, despite his medical problems, but another obstacle arose when his employer was reluctant to lose him and interceded with the First Presidency to have LeGrand's call deferred for some months. At LeGrand's request, however, the decision was reversed, and he left as originally scheduled.

Although he was bothered with his hip problems, sometimes unable to sleep, and tormented by fleas, LeGrand displayed an optimism that became a lifelong trademark: "Be habitually cheerful," he wrote to himself. "Don't be ever plaintively whining and discontentedly murmuring, and this both for your own sake and those about you. Let your face and general demeanor be like sunshine and not like a cloudy day, east wind, or a damp blanket."

In April 1906, when European Mission president Heber J. Grant arrived to visit the Holland mission, LeGrand handed him a telegram stating that three vacancies in the Quorum of the Twelve had been filled by Richards, Whitney, and McKay. "I wonder who this man Richards is," said Elder Grant. He and LeGrand both felt that it must be LeGrand's father, and they were right. George F. Richards had been called and eventually became president of the Twelve.

"My Father's
Harsh Discipline"

A young boy had a speech impediment when he first learned to talk. He could not pronounce his r's and had trouble with his g's. He said "bed" for "bread" and "dull" for "girl." Because of this difficulty, his older brother Bud, who called the boy Dutch, began teasing him. As Dutch later recalled, Bud was a practical joker who "had me in trouble most of the time."

When Bud taught Dutch to ride a donkey, he said, "Dutch, you know you don't ride a donkey like you ride a horse; you always get on backwards, and when you get on you lean forward and take hold of the donkey's flank, and he will know what to do." Dutch did as he was instructed and was promptly bucked off. Another time the two brothers were chasing a weasel that ran into its burrow. After failing to dig the weasel out with spades, Bud said, "Dutch, I think I can hear him down there. We're getting close to him. Maybe you had better reach in and see what he is doing." Again, Dutch did what he was told and suffered the consequences, bearing a scar on his finger for the rest of his life.

Dutch sought revenge after reading a story about a man who died, was buried, and came to life again. One night Dutch asked Bud to read the ghost story. When Bud got to the scariest part, Dutch said, "Leave your book now and we'll go to bed." Bud reluctantly agreed and the boys walked out to a barn where they slept. Dutch had arranged for a cousin in a sheet to be standing at the bottom of the stairs. Bud screamed when he saw what he thought was a ghost, but Dutch said, "I'll show you there's no ghost there," and walked unafraid down the dark stairs. They got in bed and Bud covered his head. "Uncover your head," said Dutch. "You'll see there are no ghosts here." Dutch uncovered his head to see the ghost standing at the foot of his bed.

Dutch explained: "He let out another unearthly scream, covered his head again, and began to pray. I felt very guilty because he told the Lord all the bad things he had done and promised never to do any more."

Casting a shadow over these innocent times was the fiery temperament of the boys' father. "He was a stern disciplinarian, having been raised in the old school of the pioneers," Dutch wrote. "It meant little to him to chastise any of his children rather severely." The father sometimes slapped Bud to the ground. "This also happened to me a few times," said Dutch.

Indeed, such attitudes were common enough that Brigham Young had once warned, "Kindness, love and affection are the best rod. . . . I can pick out scores of men in this congregation who have driven their children from them by using the wooden rod."

Dutch wrote that his mother was loyal to her husband and "upheld him in many of the things he did but was heartbroken by his severe discipline and unruly temper." Remembering her, Dutch wrote, "My mother's influence, her faith in me, and her tender feelings for all of her fourteen children . . . inspired me to be and do the best that I could."

Dutch also had an ally in his older sister Lillie. Once she stepped in between Dutch and his angry father. "Don't you dare touch my little brother!" she said, holding up her hands.

"Although I admired my father and loved him in a way, I never felt intimate or close to him," wrote Dutch. "Even up to the time of his death, his awful temper and quick tongue alienated practically all the members of his family from him."

Though Hugh B. Brown had a hard time speaking in his childhood, he eventually became one of the outstanding orators in the history of the Church. "I traveled with B. H. Roberts on many occasions," Hugh wrote. "He became my ideal so far as public speaking was concerned."

Speaking of his father, Hugh said, "I would not want to leave the impression that my father was not a good man. He loved his family sincerely and did everything he could for us, but he disciplined us severely and wanted our prompt and immediate obedience to any of his orders." Hugh's father, Homer Manley Brown, had no doubt been influenced by his own father, Homer Brown, who was, according to President Brown's biographers, Eugene Campbell and Richard Poll, "also a hard, dictatorial, self-sufficient type of man. Consulting with his wife was below his dignity. . . . Hugh's paternal grandfather, Homer, was as severe and rugged as the Utah wilderness. A polygamist with three wives, he lost the first, Sarah Ann, by divorce, after she had borne ten children, and shortly before his death he was excommunicated from the Church after an altercation with his bishop. Homer was a hard worker, a good speaker, an excellent dancer and a good mixer, well liked by many who knew him, but had an abrasive character. President Brown believed that this background may have accounted for his own father's harshness, bad temper, and lack of Church activity, although he asserts that his father 'had a great faith in the Brethren, was loyal to them and believed them to be prophets of God.' His father was especially fond of Wilford Woodruff, his neighbor in the Salt Lake Valley for some time."

Perhaps Hugh was responding to this chapter in his family history when he later wrote: "There is no room for bossism in married life, or for petty tyranny, where one or the other of the parents exercises unrighteous control or dominion. . . . "

TURNING DOWN
A CHANCE TO PLAY
PROFESSIONAL BASEBALL

Born just after the turn of the twentieth century, a boy growing up in Salt Lake City became an avid baseball player. He knew the names of the baseball heroes of his day—Honus Wagner, Ty Cobb, Christy Mathewson—and longed to someday play professional baseball himself. He played both pitcher and shortstop at West High School.

In 1922, the nineteen-year-old young man was called on a mission to the Eastern States. He served as supervising elder for the New York District at a time when Babe Ruth, recently traded from the Boston Red Sox to the New York Yankees, was making big news in New York.

After returning from his mission in 1924, he received an offer to play pro baseball and even signed a contract. About the same time, however, he was called to serve as a counselor in a bishopric. Sacrificing his hopes of competing in pro baseball, he withdrew from the contract and devoted himself to church and educational responsibilities. He must have followed the New York Yankees with a mixture of excitement and regret as they established one of the greatest teams in history in 1927. One of their key players, the soft-spoken Lou Gehrig, was the same age as this young man.

As he matured, he retained a special feeling for young people. When he was serving as bishop of the Monument Park Ward in Salt Lake City, David O. McKay, then first counselor in the First Presidency, made an unscheduled visit to a sacrament meeting to acknowledge the concern the ward had shown for its youth.

Speaking of the impromptu visit by President McKay, Alvin R. Dyer recalled: "He said he had come of his own will because he had learned of the success we had had in holding our young people. His visit to those who were there will never be forgotten, and to me it was the real beginning of an appreciation for a great man, truly a prophet of God who is inspired and is still at the helm of this Church."

When he turned down the chance to play professional baseball, Alvin was choosing spiritual priorities over worldly pursuits for the second time. Along with playing on the West High School baseball team, he had sung in a popular vocal quartet, and the foursome was offered a contract to tour with a vaudeville group for forty-two weeks. But when Alvin's bishop called him on a mission, Alvin gave up the musical opportunity as well.

Alvin married fellow West High student May Elizabeth Jackson, and they had two children, Gloria May Klein and Brent Rulon Dyer. Alvin became successful in the heating and ventilating business before being called as president of the Central States Mission in the mid-1950s.

Alvin Dyer was called as an assistant to the Quorum of the Twelve in 1958. He shared a special friendship with President David O. McKay, and in 1967 President McKay ordained him an apostle. Elder Dyer did not serve in the Quorum of the Twelve, but he was called as an additional counselor to President McKay in 1968. (During this time, Hugh B. Brown and N. Eldon Tanner were first and second counselors in the First Presidency, with Joseph Fielding Smith and Thorpe B. Isaacson also serving as additional counselors.) Elder Dyer died in 1977 at the age of seventy-four.

ARRESTED
IN SEATTLE

Ayoung man with musical interests taught himself to play the marimba and soon began performing at church and school programs. "Most orchestras were not large enough to have a marimba player unless he doubled on other instruments," he later commented, "so I commenced to play drums as well. As I played more and more on a professional basis, I started to play saxophone and clarinet and later added the trumpet."

The young musician, who already played the piano and the violin, soon formed his own group and began playing at dances, private parties, restaurants, wedding receptions, and at church and civic gatherings. Although they initially played in the Boise, Idaho, area, they soon began traveling. On one trip they were aboard a ship that docked in Seattle, Washington. They stayed overnight with friends but were in for a surprise when they returned to the ship the next morning:

"Police officers came aboard with warrants for our arrest. We were put in a police car and taken to the police station in Seattle without knowing why we were arrested. After we got there, officers interrogated each of us and we learned there had been a burglary in Boise and a number of musical instruments stolen. We were prime suspects until it was learned that we had left Boise before the burglary occurred. After an exchange of telegrams to verify this fact, they turned us loose. I tried to persuade the police to take us back to the ship, but they were tough and wouldn't do anything to help us, so we went in a taxi. Because we had been taken away and were not on board when the customs officials cleared the removal of baggage and possessions, ours had been gathered up and locked in a warehouse."

The next morning, Howard W. Hunter and his companions managed to retrieve their bags from customs. After remaining in Seattle for a few days and even playing at a hotel, they purchased an inexpensive Oldsmobile and began the journey back to Boise. They saw the sights along the way and played at a hotel in Portland, Oregon. Two days out of Portland, however, the old car gave out, and the musicians stayed overnight with a farmer and his family until one of their fathers could pick them up.

On Friday, 11 March 1927, after a tour of ten weeks, they arrived home in Boise. "It was early in the morning when we got to Boise," Howard wrote. "I called Mother and Dad and they came to get me. Home never looked as good to me as it did when we got there. This is the first time I have been away for more than a few days and I was glad to be back after a trip nearly half way around the world."

Howard, then nineteen years old, was surprised to learn that his father, John William Hunter, had been baptized while Howard was away. A week later, they attended their first priesthood meeting together. (Because of his father's wishes that Howard make up his own mind about religion, Howard had not been baptized until he was twelve, though he was active in the Church throughout his boyhood.)

The first president of the Church to be born in the twentieth century, Howard W. Hunter was called as an apostle in 1959 at the age of fifty-one. "Tears came to my eyes and I could not speak," he said of the call from President David O. McKay. "I have never felt so completely humbled as when I sat in the presence of this great, sweet, kindly man—the prophet of the Lord."

"I Had the Pernicious Habit of Smoking Cigarettes"

Born near Nauvoo in 1840, a boy named Marion was only eight years old when he drove a yoke of cattle and a wagon across the plains from Winter Quarters to Salt Lake City. The skills he acquired on the trek served him well: three years later he managed a herd of stock from Salt Lake to Southern California, where his family and several others established the community of San Bernardino.

By his early teens, Marion was an expert horseman and teamster. During the mid-1850s, he made sixteen trips across the desert from San Bernardino to Salt Lake City and back.

The freighters Marion worked with were a rough group. "I had the pernicious habit of smoking cigarettes fairly well fastened upon me," he later said. "It gave my father and mother very much concern lest one bad habit should be followed by another. The Mexicans of that region were expert smokers, and would pass volumes of smoke out by the nose which, to such boys as me, appeared to be a very great accomplishment, and I strove to do likewise, or like-*foolish*, and succeeded."

Marion tried to quit, and his father, who had been ordained an apostle in 1842, offered "a number-one horse and saddle and outfit" as an incentive, but Marion failed despite the inducement. His eventual victory came several years later. Half a century after that, as an apostle himself, he frequently pled with Church members to obey the Word of Wisdom.

An expert horseman throughout his life, Francis M. Lyman (who went by Marion) showed particular skill lassoing wild horses. "He was an expert at this business, and could lay the rope around the front feet of the animals to perfection, often taking ten in a stretch without a miss."

Noted Church historian Andrew Jenson commented that Francis's first twenty years were "truly astonishing. He was frontiersman at birth and baby-hood; pioneer, teamster, and bull-whacker at eight; herdsman and cowboy at eleven; learning a trade at thirteen; plowing the trackless deserts as a leader and captain at sixteen; married at seventeen; exploring the wilds of Colorado at eighteen; a Seventy and a missionary at twenty; with farming, attending school, presiding over improvement associations, building the log cabin of the pioneer, as incidents thrown here and there in between."

Francis persisted in his efforts to stop smoking and conquered tobacco for good when he was twenty-five. Twelve years later, in 1877, he was called to preside over the stake in Tooele, Utah. In 1880, at age forty, he explored Southern Utah, Arizona, and New Mexico with Apostle Erastus Snow and others. During the journey, Francis happened to see a copy of the *Deseret News* and learned he had been sustained at general conference as a new member of the Quorum of the Twelve.

Elder Lyman stressed the Word of Wisdom throughout his thirty-six-year ministry as an apostle. In a typical address in 1906, he posed these questions: "What converts have been made? What reformation has been made? What young men have been reformed from intemperance, from use of tobacco, from profanity, infidelity, and brought into the fold?"

"BEDLAM AND REVOLUTION"

Their senior year in high school, a young man who was student body president and his friends were present at an assembly on the last day of March when the principal issued a warning: "We have had some pretty raw things pulled off here in the school on April Fool's Day, but I want to tell you that's passed. We've outgrown such nonsense and it will not be tolerated. We hold school tomorrow as usual."

The boys took the warning as a challenge and plotted to miss school the next day. Word spread, and when the students gathered for an assembly the next day, hardly a boy was present. "The boys had gone up the mountain in hayracks with lunches to ride the flume all day. [The principal] took the podium, looked down at this assembly of girls, and burned red hot. He expelled the boys, cancelled their sports trip . . . , ruled out graduation that year for senior boys, and demanded an apology if any of them expected ever to set foot in school again."

When the boys showed up for school the next day, the principal promptly ordered them off the grounds. They left together and wandered to an old livery stable, where someone snapped a picture of thirty-two of them in front of a huge Bull Durham tobacco sign. "That Bull Durham background was evidence of bedlam and revolution," the young man later joked.

The principal had demanded an apology; the boys weren't sure they wanted to offer one. Finally a teacher came by and took the student body president aside. "You've had your fun," he said. "Now go and beg forgiveness. Take your medicine and come back to school." The young man and his friends followed the advice and apologized.

The boys begged the pardon of the staff and administration at a faculty meeting, and they signed a statement promising not to repeat their prank. When they graduated, they gave the school a gift—a pillar listing the names of the twenty-one graduates. Among them were Ralph Bilby, who became a prominent attorney, and Jesse Udall, a future Arizona Supreme Court justice. Said one of them: "I doubted the advisability then of us having a monument put up here and our names inscribed in granite, but after I've seen how important we are I've kind of concluded it was the right thing to do."

At the top of the list was the name of the student body president, Spencer W. Kimball. "Though he would later write of his part in the prank as being 'to my shame, I suppose,' he would take pleasure in telling the story to his children and grandchildren."

One of Spencer's pleasures in high school was playing on the basketball team. His coach was bold enough to challenge the University of Arizona to a game. Years later, Spencer recorded the result:

"It is a great occasion. Many people came tonight who have never been before. . . . They came in large numbers tonight. Our court is not quite regulation. We are used to it, our opponents not. I have special luck with my shots tonight and the ball goes through the hoop again and again and the game ends with our High School team the victors against the college team. I have piled up the most points through the efforts of the whole team protecting me and feeding the ball to me. I am on the shoulders of the big fellows of the Academy. They are parading me around the hall to my consternation and embarrassment. I like basketball. I would rather play this game than eat."

A Young Mother
and Her Son Survive

Born in a log cabin in 1878, Sarah was the daughter of pioneers who helped colonize Franklin, the first white settlement in Idaho. She attended the local Latter-day Saint academy and went on to teach at the community school. She had dark eyes and thick black hair, she loved to sing, and she acquired the nickname "little mother" because of the concern she showed for friends. At seventeen she completed an advanced sewing course in Logan, Utah, and was known as an excellent seamstress the rest of her life.

Two of Sarah's best friends were twin girls. She fell in love with and married their older brother. The couple purchased a two-room home and began running a forty-acre livestock farm. A year after their marriage, Sarah experienced extreme complications giving birth to her first child, a son. "There is no hope for the child, but I think we can save the mother," the country doctor informed the husband.

But the husband's mother and wife's mother were both present, and they did not despair over the apparently lifeless infant. Their grandson later related: "The faith of my father, the administrations of the priesthood and the quick action of my two grandmothers, placing me first in a pan of cold water, and then warm water, alternating, brought forth a husky yell, to the joy of all."

The two grandmothers had saved the life of a future apostle.

Just a few years later, Sarah Dunkley Benson and her husband, George, parents of Ezra Taft Benson, faced a crisis when they had only fifty dollars to their name but owed that same amount to the bank and also in tithing. Although defaulting on the loan would jeopardize the home and farm, they determined to attend tithing settlement and pay their tithing in full. As they were returning home after meeting with the bishop, they met a neighbor who offered to buy a hay derrick George had built. They agreed on a price of $50.00, and the Bensons were able to pay their bank loan.

When George was called on a mission to the Midwest states in 1912, Sarah, then expecting her eighth child, again demonstrated her faith. She fully supported her husband's mission call and trained her children, including thirteen-year-old Ezra, to help her with the chores. George Taft Benson III was born soon after his father departed for Chicago, and mother and child were both seriously ill, but Sarah did not inform her husband at the time, for fear of interfering with his missionary work. When letters arrived from the mission field, Sarah gathered the children and read the letters aloud, building a love of missionary work in her family. All eleven children later served missions.

"Sarah's love of singing carried over into her home. In times of work and relaxation, her lovely voice filled the home with warmth and pleasant melodies. She sang while she cooked, cleaned, and sewed on her treadle machine, and while she rocked her babies to sleep. One of her favorite songs was 'Have I Done Any Good in the World Today?'"

There was joy in the family when Ezra, who had received a master's degree in agricultural economics in 1927, was named head of the University of Idaho's newly organized Department of Agricultural Economics and Marketing in 1931. The future looked bright, but a year later Sarah was diagnosed with cancer. The doctors did their best, and she was operated on in Salt Lake City, but she died on 1 June 1933. She was fifty-four years old.

At the time of Sarah's passing, Ezra's younger brother George Taft, who had been born while his father was on a mission, was serving a mission himself. When he left for the mission field, his mother's last words had been "George, no matter what happens at home, I want you to stay and finish your mission." True to Sarah's wishes, George remained and completed his call.

President David O. McKay, then serving as a counselor to President Heber J. Grant, was among the speakers at Sarah's funeral. He had been Ezra's mission president in Great Britain. He concluded his talk by saying, "With all my heart I say, God bless Brother Benson and those brothers and sisters who mourn. It is something to have known and to have lived with and loved such a noble person."

George Sr. died the next year from appendicitis. Ezra thus lost both parents by the time he was thirty-five. He must have wished they could have been present when he was ordained a high priest by Charles A. Callis and set apart as a counselor in the Boise Stake presidency in 1935.

LED BY THE SPIRIT:
MODERN MIRACLES

"Capsized into the Dashing, Foaming Sea"

On the first of March, 1864, a group of five men left Salt Lake City to travel to San Francisco and then to Hawaii to preach the gospel. They traveled by stage to California and at one point saw an unarmed man shot and killed, but the stage did not stop to allow them to investigate.

The treacherous pass at the Sierra Nevada Mountains was covered with snow. "Sitting in the coach," one man wrote, "by inclining the head a little to one side, one could gaze down into the vast depths below, conscious that the wheels of the vehicle were often within a few inches of the terrible gulf; consequently, the slipping of the wheels, the least blunder of a horse, or a strap or buckle giving way, or the least carelessness of the driver, would plunge the whole outfit over the rocky crags into the abyss below. The danger was increased by the ice and snow, and the sudden abrupt turns of the road. When we approached very slippery places, where the road frequently was barely of a sufficient width for the coach to pass between the high rocks on one side and the frightful chasm on the other, the driver, in guarding against catastrophes, would put his two spans on their utmost speed. Hour after hour, as we thus drove on, particular points in the road were pointed out to us, where coaches had whirled down precipices and every occupant had been killed. These nerve-stirring recitals caused us more seriously to realize the gravity of our situation and our dependence on God for the preservation of our lives; and we truly felt grateful for our deliverance, and breathing more freely, felt our pulses restored to their normal state as we dismounted from the coach on the western slope of the Sierra Nevada Mountains."

Ironically, the greatest danger still lay ahead. They arrived in Honolulu on 27 March and sailed for Lahaina—on the island of Maui—two days later on the schooner *Nettie Merrill*. On the morning of 31 March, they came to anchor about a mile north of the small harbor at Lahaina. The sea was rough, and the captain decided to take the passengers to the harbor in a small freight boat that contained "some barrels and boxes, the captain, a white man, two or three native passengers, and the boat's crew, who were also natives."

However, one of the five men had traveled back and forth between the islands of Lanai and Maui many times and was convinced they should not try to land. In the words of his biographer, the twenty-five-year-old elder "pled earnestly with them, but he was a young man, and the brethren felt it was his place to take counsel, not to give it; moreover, being unacquainted with the nature of the sea at this place, they did not feel the anxiety which the younger man felt."

Although the others decided to go ahead, the young man "stoutly refused to go, leaving a feeling in the minds of his brethren that he was disobedient to counsel." He even volunteered to go by himself and return with a better boat, but the offer was rejected.

The young man declared, "If you, by the authority of the Priesthood of God, which you hold, tell me to get into that boat and attempt to land, I will do so, but unless you command me in the authority of the Priesthood, I will not do so, because it is not safe to attempt to land in a small boat while this storm is raging."

The others declined to issue such an order; the young man stayed behind, and the four others entered the boat. One man told what happened as they rowed toward shore: "As we approached the reef it was evident to me that the surf was running higher than we anticipated. I called the captain's attention to the fact. We were running quartering across the waves, and I suggested that we change our course so as to run at right angles with them. He replied that he did not think there was any danger, and our course was not changed. We went but a little further, when a heavy swell struck the boat and carried us before it about fifty yards. When the swell passed it left us in a trough between two huge waves. It was too late to retrieve our error, and we must run our chances. When the second swell struck the boat, it raised the stern so high that the steerman's oar was out of the water, and he lost control of the boat. It rode on the swell a short distance and swung around just as the wave began to break up. We were almost instantly capsized into the dashing, foaming sea."

Fearing he would be injured by the edge of the boat or the barrels, this man plunged headfirst into the water. When he surfaced, he saw that the boat was upside down, with barrels, hats, and umbrellas floating in every direction. As he swam for the boat, he saw a second man doing the same. They seized the edge of the boat. "[A third member of the party] came up on the opposite side of the boat from [us]. He was considerably strangled, but succeeded in securing a hold on the boat. A short time afterwards the captain was discovered, about fifty yards from us. Two sailors, one on each side, succeeded in keeping him on the surface, although life was apparently extinct."

Though they had survived, the three men, now about four hundred yards from shore, were alarmed that they could not see the fourth member of their group. Several of the natives began diving in an attempt to find him. "The people, as soon as they discovered our circumstances, manned a life boat and hurried to the rescue. We were taken into the boat, when the crew wanted to row for the shore, and pick up the captain by the way. We told them that one of our friends was yet missing, and we did not want to leave."

The natives saw that a second boat was about to reach the captain, and they agreed to help search for the missing man, Apostle Lorenzo Snow. Alma L. Smith, William W. Cluff, and Apostle Ezra T. Benson were extremely worried about their companion. As Elder Cluff put it, "the anxiety was intense. The natives were, evidently, doing all in their power. Finally, one of them, in edging himself around the capsized boat, must have felt Brother Snow with his feet and pulled him, at least, partly from under it, as the first I saw of Brother Snow was his hair floating upon the water around one end of the capsized boat. . . . His body was stiff, and life apparently extinct."

As the natives rowed for shore, Elders Cluff and Smith laid Elder Snow across their laps and "quietly administered to him and asked the Lord to spare his life, that he might return to his family and home." When they reached the beach, they laid him face down and rolled him back and forth to expel the water he had swallowed. Next they washed his face with camphor. "We did not only what was customary in such cases, but also what the Spirit seemed to whisper to us."

They tried for some time, "without any indications of returning life." Some bystanders said that nothing more could be done, but the elders felt impressed to try what was essentially artificial respiration, though they had no knowledge of the concept. "This we persevered in until we succeeded in inflating his lungs. After a little, we perceived very faint indications of returning life." Approximately one hour after the boat had capsized, Elder Snow finally regained consciousness.

Lorenzo Snow later recorded his perspective of the accident: "A short distance behind us I saw an immense surf, thirty or forty feet high, rush towards us swifter than a race horse. We had scarcely a moment for reflection before the huge mass was upon us. In an instant our boat, with its contents, as though it were a feather, was hurled into a gulf of briny waters, and all was under this rolling seething mountain wave. . . . I was confident, however, there would be some way of escape; that the Lord would provide the means, for it was not possible that my life and mission were thus to terminate. This reliance on the Lord banished fear, and inspired me up to the last moment of consciousness."

The next thing Elder Snow remembered was a very small light, "the smallest imaginable," that appeared and then vanished. It continued to appear and fade, getting brighter each time, until he finally recognized Elder Cluff's voice. "You have been drowned," he said, "the boat upset in the surf."

Elder Snow's first thought was of his fellow missionaries. "Are you brethren all safe?" he asked. Elder Cluff replied that everyone was safe. "The emotion that was awakened in my bosom by the answer of Elder Cluff will remain with me as long as life continues," wrote Lorenzo Snow. Elder Snow was soon able to walk and appeared to have no lasting damage from the accident.

Elder Cluff then realized that he had to return to the vessel and inform Joseph F. Smith, the young man who had refused to enter the small boat with them, that they had all survived. "As I reached the deck by the rope ladder over its side, I saw at a glance that Brother Smith was under great anxiety of mind. We were both under an intensity of feeling which men usually experience only a few times in their lives. Brother Smith had been informed by a native that the captain and an elderly white man were drowned. The latter he supposed to be Brother Benson, hence his great anxiety. My own nervous system was strung up to an extreme tension by the events of the past two hours. When I told Brother Smith we were all safe, . . . we rejoiced together that through a merciful Providence, and the faith that had been bestowed upon us, we were all alive."

"The Horses Responded to Father's Good Training"

A young man related the following experience he had with his father: "On a mid-September afternoon, father decided to spend a few hours dragging some fallen, dead trees from the grove in Dry Hollow. . . . The horses, pastured in the meadow, came up to him as usual when he whistled to them, and they were soon harnessed. After procuring a long chain from the shed, I followed father with an ax to help clear paths where necessary and to chop branches from the fallen trees. The horses were nervous and excited because they had done little work during the summer, and they pulled anxiously and hard at the bits. It was no easy task for father to hold them when the first log was dislodged because they became frightened at the noise of crackling dead wood and brush. Taking the small logs first, we worked up to the largest and heaviest of the fallen timber.

" 'I don't think the team can pull this one,' I remarked.

" 'Let's saw off this top end,' replied father, 'then I believe the horses are equal to it.'

"This largest tree was water-soaked and very heavy, but the team buckled down and pulled with all their strength. As father guided them into an opening, I suddenly heard a distraught yell of 'Whoa!' and glancing up, I saw father fall to the ground. The tree had rolled toward him as he was making a turn and caught him at the back of his legs, throwing him face downward. The momentum carried the tree squarely across the calves of both legs. Fortunately, the horses responded to father's good training, and remained standing at his command of 'Whoa.' Had they continued pulling, the heavy log would have been dragged over his body, crushing him. I jumped for the reins, unhooked the doubletrees, then grabbed a long pole with the intent of using it as a lever to roll the tree from father's legs. A multitude of thoughts raced through my mind: 'How to get him to a hospital?' 'Could I lift him into a car?' 'Should I try to remove his high leather boots from mashed legs?' 'Will he faint from the pain?' And while these and other ideas kept coming, I frantically worked at the tree but was unable to budge it.

"'Keep a cool head,' remarked father. 'Turn the team around and pull the tree away from me.' As I did so, I had visions of the heavy log tearing the flesh of the legs, but I did as instructed.

"'Are you in much pain?' I asked after the tree was off his legs.

"'I think I'm all right,' he said as he rubbed his legs for a few minutes, and then to prove it, he got to his feet. It was one of the biggest surprises of my life to see him do so, for I was positive both legs had been broken.

"'We had better go immediately to the hospital in Ogden and have your legs looked at and X-rayed,' I suggested.

"'No, let's finish our job, I can take care of my bruises tonight; it is only the right one which pains, and I think it is not seriously injured.'

"So continue to work we did, and after three more hours of dragging out dead trees, father was satisfied that his objective of the afternoon had been reached.

"The next day father was in the hospital. Blood vessels in both legs had been broken, and his right leg particularly was swollen and black. Instead of complaining, he remarked, 'I was lucky to have had high boots on,—and it pays to have a team with "horse-sense"; if they hadn't stopped when I yelled "whoa," I would have been a goner.'"

The man who trained his horses so well was David O. McKay. His son Llewlyn R. McKay had been working with him the day of the accident.

David O. McKay was born in 1873 and raised on the same farm where the accident took place, in Huntsville, Utah. When David was six, his two older sisters died. One year later his father, David Sr., left on a mission to Scotland (where David Jr. himself later served as a young man).

Helping his mother run the farm, young David learned to love horses from an early age. While still a boy, he delivered the *Ogden Standard Examiner* to a local mining town and spent the round trip on horseback, reading passages from the world's great literature, a habit that manifested itself in his lifelong emphasis on education and his love of good books.

David and his wife, Emma Ray Riggs, were married in 1901. As they were raising their children, they had a horse named Star, a gentle horse that was very good with the children. Star and most of the other horses had to be sold in 1922, however, when the family left for England, where Elder McKay (who had been an apostle since 1906) presided over the European Mission.

More than two years later, after fulfilling the mission, David happened to see Star in the field of her new owner. He got out of his car and called to the horse, which ran to him and nuzzled her nose under his arm.

"You know," he said, "I think she's lonesome. She ought to be back in our pasture."

The next day he bought Star back, paying more than the selling price.

Although he suffered other accidents involving his horses, President McKay rode virtually his entire life. At the April general conference in 1963, when David O. McKay was eighty-nine, Elder William J. Critchlow Jr. told the following story, typifying the Church president's passion for horses:

"President McKay opened the pasture gate, entered alone, and closed the gate. He asked us to stand quietly back a few paces. There was neither sight nor sound of pastured animals—brush obscured our view. Advancing a few paces, he raised his voice and called: 'Sonny Boy, Sonny Boy.' For moments there was silence, and in that silence I recalled that Sonny Boy was a spirited animal—the men who shod him had warned that he could give anyone a bad time. He gave them one.

"Faintly I soon heard the sound of hoofs thudding rapidly upon the sod. The thudding strengthened, growing louder and louder and still louder; and then suddenly, two horses charged around the brush, racing neck to neck straight toward President McKay. I held my breath, fearing that they would trample him before they could check their speed. Doesn't he realize the danger? He did, he knew exactly what the horses would do; he didn't even budge; the experience was not new to him or to the horses.

"Now picture this in your minds: President McKay with his arm over Sonny Boy's neck, both horses nuzzling him. . . . I also beheld the President sweeten the greeting with sugar lumps from his pocket. The horses liked the sugar. I think they liked the President. I am very sure the President loved his horses. His arm around the neck of Sonny Boy was not intended as a show of affection; it half concealed a rope which he deftly circled around the neck to make the horse captive. Sonny Boy did not seem to mind—not much. He took the bit, gently, and made no fuss about the saddle. The President tightened the new cinches, lengthened the stirrups; then mounting without assistance, he prodded the horse into a trot which broke into a gallop as they disappeared, about as the horses came, around the brush and out of sight."

ENCIRCLED
BY LIGHT

Apopular young woman attending Utah State Agricultural
College (later Utah State University) in Logan, Utah, was driving her car one day when she saw a friend standing on the corner with
a young man she didn't recognize. She waved, and as they waved back,
she wondered who the young man was. She soon discovered he was
her friend's cousin, a farm boy who couldn't afford to attend college all
year. The two of them began dating, but their courtship was interrupted when he was called on a mission.

When he returned, he proposed, but she had now decided to serve
a mission. She was called to Hawaii, where her mother was her companion for eight months. She also served in the Hawaiian Temple.
One night as she prepared to leave, she discovered everyone else had
left the temple. To return to the mission home, she had to walk
through a thick forest and near a camp known to be dangerous.

Apprehensive about returning to the mission home alone, she
prayed before leaving the temple. "As she stepped outside, a circle of
light appeared and surrounded her. That radiance shone around and
ahead of her as she walked through the forest, past the camp, and to
the steps of the mission home, disappearing as she slipped inside."

She later said that she had felt encircled by the Lord's Spirit many
times in her life, but never so literally as that lonely night in the
islands.

When she returned from her mission, Flora Amussen and Ezra Taft Benson made plans to marry. "I had inherited from my father quite a portion of worldly goods in stocks and substantial dividends," Sister Benson later explained. "I turned all of this over to my widowed mother at the time of my marriage. I chose to marry a man who was rich spiritually, not materially. I preferred that whatever positions of honor or material things would come to us, we would achieve together, starting at the bottom."

Right after they were married (in September of 1926), Ezra and Flora left Utah for Ames, Iowa, where the young husband had accepted a seventy-dollar-a-month postgraduate scholarship at Iowa State College. They packed all of their belongings in a Model T pickup and spent the nights in a leaky tent as they drove east.

Ezra quickly advanced in his chosen career of agriculture, working first as a county extension agent, then as a specialist for the University of Idaho, then as executive secretary of a national farming organization. In 1952, he was shocked to learn that Dwight D. Eisenhower, a man he had never met, wanted him to serve as secretary of agriculture. Though Elder Benson was then serving in the Quorum of the Twelve, President McKay advised him to accept the position.

On several occasions, Flora hosted Mrs. Eisenhower and other prominent women. Flora and her daughters typically took care of all the preparations, not hiring outside help, and arranging for touring BYU groups to provide the music. Recalling a luncheon she hosted, Flora said: "The most exciting part was the beautiful letters we received afterward from the women, telling us what a thrill it was to experience a touch of 'Mormonism' and family cooperation and what wonderful youth the BYU singers were."

"I WOULD HAVE
ANGELS ATTEND ME"

A woman who served for thirty-three years in the general Primary was the first woman to serve on a national Boy Scout committee and to receive the Silver Buffalo award. Along with incorporating scouting into the Primary program, she oversaw the expansion of the Primary Children's Hospital and edited the *Children's Friend*. "I was responsible for anything that went in the magazine," she said. "I had to make final decisions. We did all the editing; we read all the proofs." During this time, the Primary also encouraged children to donate nickels and dimes to "send a Friend on a mission." The program was quite successful; several families told of being brought into the Church because of the magazine.

The sister noted that she had never missed a Primary assignment because of health problems. However, she once required surgery on the Saturday before April conference. She was released from the hospital on Tuesday, with her doctor reluctantly allowing her to attend Primary general conference if she would spend several days in bed immediately afterwards.

"When I got down to the Tabernacle Thursday morning," she said, "President [Harold B.] Lee was there and he'd brought Elder Sterling W. Sill and he said, 'I want to give you a blessing . . . before you go into your conference.' And he blessed me that it would be a conference such as I had never experienced and that I would have angels attend me. And truly I did. I could feel it. I conducted all the meetings and I stood in line and shook hands with two thousand Primary workers and I didn't have to go home and go to bed afterwards."

Born 1 January 1900, Lavern Watts Parmley was raised with eight brothers and said that boys were her "specialty." She took a special interest in programs for boys throughout her tenure in the general Primary.

She also worked tirelessly to improve children's health. Along with helping Primary Children's Hospital become a leading center of pediatric medicine, she served two terms as a trustee of the National Association of Children's Hospitals and Related Institutions and three terms as president of the Utah Lung Association. She was also a board member of the Utah Tuberculosis and Health Association.

Lavern, who married University of Utah physics professor Thomas J. Parmley, was called as first counselor in the general Primary presidency in 1943. She was sustained as president eight years later and served until 1974. The year of 1952 was particularly memorable because the new Primary Children's Hospital was dedicated in March, and the Cub Scouts became part of Primary in December.

After her release, Sister Parmley taught Relief Society and took an institute class. "I have not regretted my release at all," she said. "I have found so many interesting things to do. I have felt that I did the best I could while I was in the Primary in the 23 years I was in the presidency and . . . [the] ten years [I was] a counselor."

"Mother was an executive, who was focused, goal-driven, and accomplished a lot," said her daughter Fannie. "She knew what it took to make something happen. She could figure out where she was, where she wanted to be, and how to get there. That was her greatest strength. She spent little time or energy worrying about inconsequential things."

"HER SPIRIT APPARENTLY LEFT HER BODY"

A thirty-one-year-old native of Connecticut recorded the following experience: "On the afternoon of the 9th of October we . . . started upon our journey of 2,000 miles at this late season of the year, taking my wife with a suckling babe at her breast with me, to lead a company of fifty-three souls from Maine to Illinois, and to spend nearly three months in traveling in wagons, through rain, mud, snow and frost. It was such a trial as I never before had attempted during my experience as a minister of the gospel."

Within two weeks, the man, his wife, their three-month-old daughter, and several others in the company were sick. On 4 November, "a little boy of Nathaniel Homes', about six years of age, died, and we had to bury him at Westfield." As the man wrote, his wife "grew more and more distressed daily as we continued our journey. It was a terrible ordeal for a woman to travel in a wagon over rough roads, afflicted as she was. At the same time our child was also very sick.

"The 1st of December was a trying day to my soul. My wife continued to fail, and in the afternoon, about 4 o'clock, she appeared to be struck with death. I stopped my team, and it seemed as though she would breathe her last lying in the wagon. Two of the sisters sat beside her, to see if they could do anything for her in her last moments.

"I stood upon the ground, in deep affliction, and meditated. I cried unto the Lord, and prayed that she might live and not be taken from me. I claimed the promises the Lord had made unto me through the prophets and patriarchs, and soon her spirit revived, and I drove a short distance to a tavern, and got her into a room and worked over her and her babe all night, and prayed to the Lord to preserve her life.

"In the morning the circumstances were such that I was under the necessity of removing my wife from the inn, as there was so much noise and confusion at the place that she not could endure it. I carried her out to her bed in the wagon and drove two miles, when I alighted at a house and carried my wife and her bed into it, with a determination to tarry there until she either recovered her health or passed away. This was on Sunday morning, December 2nd.

"After getting my wife and things into the house and wood provided to keep up a fire, I employed my time in taking care of her. It looked as though she had but a short time to live.

"She called me to her bedside in the evening and said she felt as though a few moments more would end her existence in this life. She manifested great confidence in the cause she had embraced, and exhorted me to have confidence in God and to keep His commandments.

"To all appearances, she was dying. I laid hands upon her and prayed for her, and she soon revived and slept some during the night.

"December 3rd found my wife very low. I spent the day in taking care of her, and the following day I returned to Eaton to get some things for her. She seemed to be gradually sinking and in the evening her spirit apparently left her body, and she was dead.

"The sisters gathered around her body, weeping, while I stood looking at her in sorrow. The spirit and power of God began to rest upon me until, for the first time during her sickness, faith filled my soul, although she lay before me as one dead.

"I had some oil that was consecrated for my anointing while in Kirtland. I took it and consecrated it again before the Lord for anointing the sick. I then bowed down before the Lord and prayed for the life of my companion, and I anointed her body with the oil in the name of the Lord. I laid my hands upon her, and in the name of Jesus Christ I rebuked the power of death and the destroyer, and commanded the same to depart from her, and the spirit of life to enter her body.

"Her spirit returned to her body, and from that hour she was made whole; and we all felt to praise the name of God, and to trust in Him and to keep His commandments.

"While this operation was going on with me (as my wife related afterwards) her spirit left her body, and she saw it lying upon the bed, and the sisters weeping. She looked at them and at me, and upon her babe, and, while gazing upon this scene, two personages came into the room carrying a coffin and told her they had come for her body. One of these messengers informed her that she could have her choice: she might go to rest in the spirit world, or, on one condition she could have the privilege of returning to her tabernacle and continuing her labors upon the earth. The condition was, if she felt that she could stand by her husband, and with him pass through all the cares, trials, tribulation and afflictions of life which he would be called to pass through for the gospel's sake unto the end. When she looked at the situation of her husband and child she said: 'Yes, I will do it!'

"At the moment that decision was made the power of faith rested upon me, and when I administered unto her, her spirit entered her tabernacle, and she saw the messengers carry the coffin out at the door.

"On the morning of the 6th of December, the Spirit said to me: 'Arise, and continue thy journey!' and through the mercy of God my wife was enabled to arise and dress herself and walked to the wagon, and we went on our way rejoicing."

The recipients of this miracle were Wilford and Phoebe W. Carter Woodruff. Just a few days later, when they stopped at an inn, they learned of the sudden death of Wilford's brother, Asahel H. Woodruff. "I had anticipated a joyful meeting with this brother on the following day," wrote Wilford. "Instead of this, I only had the privilege of visiting his grave, in company with my wife, and examining a little into his business."

Wilford and Phoebe had been married in Joseph Smith's home in Kirtland in April of 1837. A month later, Wilford left on a mission, traveling through New York, into Canada, and then back into New York and eventually to his boyhood home in Avon, Connecticut. Phoebe joined him there in July, and he preached the gospel to several of his relatives. He and Phoebe then made their way toward Maine, with the tireless Wilford matter-of-factly stating, "On my arrival at Hartford, not having money to pay the fare for both of us, I paid my wife's fare to Rowley, Mass., where there was a branch of the Church . . . and I journeyed on foot.

"The first day I walked fifty-two miles, the second forty-eight, and the third day thirty-six miles, and arrived at Rowley at two o'clock, making 136 miles in a little over two and a half days."

Leaving Phoebe at her father's home in Scarborough, Maine, Wilford departed to preach the gospel in the Fox Islands, off the coast of Maine. Over the next year, Wilford baptized a number of converts on the islands and in other parts of New England, spending time with Phoebe whenever possible. On 9 August 1838, while holding meetings on Vinalhaven Island, he received a letter from Thomas B. Marsh informing him that Joseph Smith had received a revelation naming him, John E. Page, John Taylor, and Willard Richards to fill vacancies in the Quorum of the Twelve. (These men replaced William E.

M'Lellin, Luke Johnson, John F. Boynton, and Lyman E. Johnson, all of whom had been excommunicated.) Thomas B. Marsh further instructed Wilford to "come speedily to Far West [Missouri]."

"The substance of this letter had been revealed to me several weeks before, but I had not named it to any person," Wilford added.

Because the devil "was raging upon every hand," Wilford thought it imperative to take as many Saints as possible with him, necessitating the departure so late in the year.

As Phoebe had been forewarned by divine messengers, she and Wilford experienced many "cares, trials, tribulation and afflictions." They endured a severe trial a year and a half later with the death of their first child, a daughter named Sarah Emma, the same child who was with them on the journey from Maine to Illinois. Sarah Emma died in July of 1840, three days after her second birthday, while Wilford was serving a mission in England. "My Dear Wilford," wrote Phoebe, "what will be your feelings, when I say that yesterday I was called to witness the departure of our little Sarah Emma from this world. Yes, she is gone. The relentless hand of death has snatched her from my embrace."

By 1853, Wilford and Phoebe had lost four more children— Joseph, Ezra, Sarah, and Aphek, all of whom died in infancy. Frequently separated in their forty-eight years of marriage, Wilford and Phoebe were separated even in death. When Phoebe died at age seventy-eight on 10 November 1885, Wilford was prevented from attending the funeral because raids by U.S. marshals had forced him and others into hiding. (Wilford had spent time in northern Arizona and southern Utah during this self-imposed exile.) He watched the funeral procession of his first wife, and mother of their nine children, from a window in the Church Historian's Office.

SOURCES

Against All Odds: Courage in the Face of Adversity and Persecution

A Young Boy Loses His Sight
Talmage, 6–7, 239; *Improvement Era*, September 1954, 635, 660, 662. See also *Improvement Era*, July 1942, 438, 470; March 1955, 138.

"My Dear Zina Passed to Her Final Rest"
Whitney, 230–33.

"Every Heart Is Filled with Sorrow"
Vilate Kimball to Heber C. Kimball, 30 June 1844, photocopy of original letter, Vilate Kimball Papers, LDS Church Archives, cited in Madsen, 138–39. The version printed here has been edited slightly for readability. Eliza R. Snow, "Sketch of My Life," 13, typescript, LDS Church Archives, cited in Newell and Avery, 197. The arrival of the Twelve in Nauvoo: Manuscript History of Brigham Young, 171, cited in Arrington, 112. Premonitions of Heber C. Kimball: *History of the Church*, 7:132. George Q. Cannon's account: *Juvenile Instructor* 22 (29 October 1870): 174–75, cited in Arrington, 115.

A Son Taken in His Youth
Tate, 160, 162.

A Deadly Tornado
Joseph Fielding Smith to Levira Smith, 28 June 1860, LDS Church Archives, cited in Newell and Avery, 273. Michael Morse's statement concerning the translation of the Book of Mormon: see *Saints Herald* 26 (15 June 1879): 190–91.

The Dungeon Called Liberty Jail
Sidney Rigdon's speech at the dedication of the Kirtland Temple: *Latter Day Saints' Messenger and Advocate* 2 (March 1836): 276. John's visit to Liberty Jail: Rigdon, 36. Sidney's escape from Liberty Jail: Rigdon, 38. Sidney's conversion: *Times and Seasons*, 4:290; Rigdon, 24. John's conversations with his parents: Rigdon, 41–42.

Escaping the Mexican Revolution
Miner and Kimball, 20–21, 25, 27–30, 199–200, 156. Spencer and Camilla's trip to Europe: Kimball and Kimball, 165.

"I Was Called to the Bedside of My Wife"
Smith and Stewart, 243, 247–48, 249.

Killed on a Mission to the Indians
The relationship of George Albert and Bathsheba: Record Book of Bathsheba W. Smith, typescript, 33, L. Tom Perry Special Collections Library, Harold B. Lee Library,

Brigham Young University. Joseph Smith's premonition of his death: Preston Nibley, "She Knew the Prophet Joseph Smith: Part III—Bathsheba W. Smith," *Relief Society Magazine* 49 (June 1962): 410–11, cited in Peterson and Gaunt, *Elect Ladies*, 61. The true order of prayer: Andrus, 123. The trek to Winter Quarters: Tullidge, 322. Crossing the plains: Tullidge, 342. George Jr.'s death: Record Book, 33–34. George Albert's death: Bathsheba W. Smith Autobiography, 42, cited in Barbara B. Smith, 137. Emmeline B. Wells's description: Derr, 152. Susa Young Gates's description: Susa Young Gates, *History of the Young Ladies' Mutual Improvement Association*, 26–28, cited in Peterson and Gaunt, *Elect Ladies*, 75–76.

"Everything Reminded Me of Her"

Howard W. Hunter journal entries: Knowles, 265, 267–68, 268–69. Claire's death: Knowles, 269–70. Elder Faust's comments: Knowles, 271. Use of wheelchair: Knowles, 284–85. Marriage to Inis: Knowles, 291–92. President Hunter's comments on becoming Church president: Todd, 4–5.

"Friends at First Are Friends Again at Last": The Fellowship of the Saints

"A Fully Satisfactory Golf Shot"

Golf story: Talmage, 225–28. Bicycle experience: Talmage, 139–40.

"A Beloved Leader Leaves Instructions for His Own Funeral"

Funeral instructions: Richards, 136–37. J. Golden's childhood: *Improvement Era,* October 1938, 590. Hugh's childhood: Firmage, 5. J. Golden on Hugh's call as mission president: Campbell and Poll, 121. Hugh's tribute: Richards, 124–25.

An Apostle, An Entrepreneur, and a U.S. President

J. Willard Marriott's childhood: *Ensign,* December 1972, 86. President Kimball's childhood: *Ensign,* November 1975, 13. J. Willard Marriott to Spencer W. Kimball, 18 October 1974, J. Willard Marriott Collection, Special Collections, University of Utah.

A Friend to Children

Promise given to Joan: Goates, *Harold B. Lee,* 358. President McKay's comments: Goates, 360. President Lee's comments: Goates, 362.

A Lost Sheep Returns to the Fold

Edson Don Carlos Smith Papers, LDS Church Archives.

A Friendship Survives

Amy's remembrance of Eliza R. Snow and Zina D. H. Young: Amy Brown Lyman, *In Retrospect: Autobiography of Amy Brown Lyman* (Salt Lake City: General Board of Relief Society, 1945), 38, cited in Peterson and Gaunt, *Elect Ladies,* 130–31. Emmeline B. Harris quote: Relief Society General Board Minutes, 10 December 1913, cited in Derr, Cannon, and Beecher, 189. Joseph F. Smith's comments: Derr, Cannon, and Beecher, 215. Susa Young Gates's opinions: Susa Young Gates to the Presidency and Board of the Relief Society, 4 November 1919, cited in Derr, Cannon, and Beecher, 216; Susa Young Gates to Elizabeth Caridge McCune, 17 November 1919, cited in Madsen and Stovall, 130. Quote from historians: Ibid. Susa Young Gates's comment on the conflict: Susa Young Gates to the Presidency and Board of the Relief Society, 4

November 1919, cited in Madsen and Stovall, 131. Susa Young Gates on times past: Van Wagoner and Walker, 92. Amy Brown Lyman on her mother: Lyman, 7, cited in Peterson and Gaunt, *Elect Ladies*, 129–30. Emmeline B. Wells to Mrs. Amy Brown Lyman, 6 October 1909, cited in Madsen and Stovall, 132.

"I Know Him Better Than Any Other Man"

George Beard to the First Presidency and Apostles of The Church of Jesus Christ of Latter-day Saints, 10 October 1933, L. Tom Perry Special Collections Library, Harold B. Lee Library, Brigham Young University. Nephi Jensen Journal, cited in Bennett, 51.

Eyewitnesses to History: Encounters with Well-Known Individuals

A Letter to Helen Keller

David O. McKay's comments: Middlemiss, 121. Swedenborgian beliefs: Reese, 559. Levi Edgar Young's comments: Conference Report, April 1940, 102. Helen Keller to J. Reuben Clark Jr., 14 March 1941, J. Reuben Clark Collection, L. Tom Perry Special Collections Library, Harold B. Lee Library, Brigham Young University. J. Reuben Clark Jr. to Helen Keller, 22 March 1941, L. Tom Perry Special Collections Library. Lowell Thomas to J. Reuben Clark Jr., 12 July 1954, L. Tom Perry Special Collections Library. President Clark on socialism: Quoted in Ezra Taft Benson, Conference Report, April 1963, 111–12. Quote from Helen Keller: Keller, 374.

Pearl S. Buck's Book of Hope

Pearl S. Buck's feelings about the war: Conn, 237; Pearl S. Buck to Mrs. Heber J. Grant, 8 July 1940, J. Reuben Clark Jr. Collection, L. Tom Perry Special Collections Library, Harold B. Lee Library, Brigham Young University. George Albert Smith's comments: Conference Report, October 1950, 134.

Hosting Nikita Khrushchev

Dew, *Ezra Taft Benson*, 339–44.

A Visit from Jane Addams

Jane Addams's visit: Lyman, 113–14. Amy's first interest in social work: Van Wagoner and Walker, 169. Amy's testimony: Lyman, 160–61.

Meeting Einstein at Princeton

Henry Eyring's comments about Einstein: Kimball, "Science and Religion," 107–8. Einstein at Princeton: Clark, 506–12. Remembrance by student at oral exam: Kimball, "Harvey Fletcher and Henry Eyring," 82.

A Gift for Dwight Eisenhower

O'Brien, 248.

A Friendship with Susan B. Anthony

Role of *Woman's Exponent*: *Woman's Exponent* 1 (1 June 1871): 4, cited in Garr, Cannon, and Cowan, 1355. Quote from Emmeline B. Wells: Wells, Diary, 4 January 1878, cited in Madsen, 137. B. H. Roberts quote: Ludlow, 1572.

A National Hero Defends the Church

Collier's (15 April 1911): 28, 36.

"Ye That Embark in the Service of God": Living and Preaching the Gospel

"One of the Dearest Friends We Will Ever Know"

George Albert Smith's meeting with President Truman: Conference Report, October 1947, 5–6. Ezra Taft Benson's experience in Europe: Dew, *Ezra Taft Benson*, 219. Statistics on items sent: Rudd, 249–51. Ezra Taft Benson on George Albert Smith: Conference Report, April 1951, 46. Comments from Archbishop Athenagoris: *Improvement Era*, January 1948, 5. John A. Widtsoe on George Albert Smith: Conference Report, April 1951, 99. Comments from Irene Jones: Conference Report, April 1951, Solemn Assembly, 173.

Telling the Story of Brigham Young

Leah Widtsoe's reminiscences: Oral History Interview, 11 February 1965, typescript, 11–16, L. Tom Perry Special Collections Library, Harold B. Lee Library, Brigham Young University. Susa's description of herself: Van Wagoner and Walker, 190. Susa's description of Brigham Young: Arrington, 332. Franklin Harris's comments: Quoted in Josephson, *Improvement Era*, January 1953, 60.

Four Decades of Service

Belle S. Spafford, "My Feelings upon Being Released as President of Relief Society," typescript, L. Tom Perry Special Collections Library, Harold B. Lee Library, Brigham Young University.

"I Seemed to See a Council in Heaven"

Heber J. Grant, Conference Report, April 1941, 4–6.

Three Generations of Apostle Missionaries

George F. Richards's dream: George F. Richards, Conference Report, October 1946, 139. Comments from missionary: Tate, 173. LeGrand on his call: Tate, 243. LeGrand on writing: Tate, 234–35. President Monson's comments: Tate, 237.

Remembering Joseph's Family

Brigham Young to Katharine Smith Salisbury, 17 May 1871, typescript, L. Tom Perry Special Collections Library, Harold B. Lee Library, Brigham Young University. Visits of George Albert Smith and Victor Bean: Anderson, *Ensign*, March 1979, 44. Katharine's remembrance of Joseph: Katharine Smith Salisbury to Dear Sisters, 10 March 1886, cited in Vogel, 1:521–22. Visit of Elder Bean, Anderson, 44.

The Cane Creek Massacre

B. H. Roberts's account of the light in room: B. H. Roberts, Biographical Notes, 271–72, cited in Madsen, 147; hearing of the murders: Biographical Notes, 213, cited in Madsen, 147; being prompted he would be able to secure the bodies: John Nicholson, "The Utah Conspiracy," cited in Madsen, 146. J. Golden Kimball's account: Conference Report, October 1933, 43. B. H. Roberts's prevailing upon J. Golden Kimball: Richards, 40–41; concluding remarks on the massacre: Madsen, 149–51. J. Golden Kimball on B. H. Roberts: Conference Report, October 1933, 42–43.

The First Sister Missionaries

Mangum, 62–65.

A Letter from a Future Church President

George Albert Smith to Mrs. Grace E. Callis, 10 October 1933, L. Tom Perry Special Collections Library, Harold B. Lee Library, Brigham Young University. Richard L. Evans's comments: Conference Report, October 1945, 43. Richard S. Watson's comments: Quoted in Jones, *Improvement Era*, June 1951, 463.

"When I Was Young": Life-Changing Moments

The Old Prophet Mason

Wilford's account of the prophet Mason: Woodruff, *Leaves from My Journal*, 1–4. Wilford's reflections on hearing sermons by Elders Pratt, Rigdon, and Hyde: Woodruff, *Journal* (April–May 1834), 1:8–9; Woodruff, "Autobiography," 38–39, cited in Alexander, 135. Quote from Thomas G. Alexander: Alexander, 139. Wilford's reflections on Zion's Camp: *Leaves from My Journal*, 6, and "Autobiography," 46; cited in Alexander, 139.

An Apostle Recalls His First Mission

Matthew Cowley missionary journal, L. Tom Perry Special Collections Library, Harold B. Lee Library, Brigham Young University. Later reminiscences: Cowley, 162, 437, 418. Matthew Cowley's patriarchal blessing: *Improvement Era*, November 1945, 656. Experience of David O. McKay: Zobell Jr., *Improvement Era*, October 1954, 730.

Heartbreak in Nauvoo

Nauvoo diary excerpts: L. Tom Perry Special Collections Library, Brigham Young University, cited in Madsen, 45–48. Brigham Young's instructions to store grain: *Deseret News*, 7 September 1940, 1, cited in Rudd, 84. Emmeline's marriage to Daniel H. Wells: Van Wagoner and Walker, 383.

Studying with World-Renowned Scholars

Widtsoe, 54–58, 37. Jacobson, 20.

"I Was Left to Wallow in My Blood"

Lucy Mack Smith's account: Lavina Fielding Anderson, 310–16. Joseph's account is from his 1839 history, Joseph Smith Papers, LDS Church Archives, cited in Jesse, 268–69. Bushman, 40–41.

An Accident-Prone Boy

Tate, 12–14, 31, 41, 47–48.

"Joseph Smith Called at My Father's"

Eliza R. Snow, 2–7. Joseph Smith was the "choice of my life": *Woman's Exponent* 15 (1 August 1886): 37. First Presidency statement: The First Presidency of the Church, "The Origin of Man," 1909.

"My Father's Harsh Discipline"

Campbell and Poll, 4–15, 21. Firmage, 1–4, 16–17.

The Mother of a Future Prophet Accepts the Gospel

Mary Grant Judd, "Rachel Ridgway Ivins Grant," *Relief Society Magazine*, April 1943, 228–29, cited in Hartshorn, 18–19. Mention of Joseph Smith: Cannon and Whittaker, 21. Nauvoo description of Rachel: Emmeline B. Wells as quoted by Judd, 229, cited in Cannon and Whittaker, 22.

Turning Down a Chance to Play Professional Baseball
Visit by President McKay: Conference Report, April 1968, 79.

Arrested in Seattle
Knowles, 46–57, 144–45.

"I Had the Pernicious Habit of Smoking Cigarettes"
Tobacco habit: Van Wagoner and Walker, 273. Skill with rope: Jenson, 1:136. Andrew Jenson's summary: Ibid. Elder Lyman's comment on the Word of Wisdom: *Improvement Era*, July 1906, 736.

"Bedlam and Revolution"
Kimball and Kimball, 65–68.

A Young Mother and Her Son Survive
President Benson's account of his birth: Quoted in Flake, 123. His mother's love of singing: Arrington and Madsen, 205. George's mission: Ibid., 206. President McKay's comments: Ibid., 207.

Led by the Spirit: Modern Miracles

"Capsized into the Dashing, Foaming Sea"
Trip through Sierra Nevada Mountains: Snow, *Biography*, 275. Small freight boat: Ibid., 276. Young elder pleads with others, resulting in accident: Joseph Fielding Smith, 212–14; Snow, 277–78.

"The Horses Responded to Father's Good Training"
Son's account: McKay, 160–62. Story of Star: Ibid., 126–27. Elder Critchlow's comments: Conference Report, April 1963, 30.

Encircled by Light
Rodriguez, 14–19.

"I Would Have Angels Attend Me"
Peterson and Gaunt, *The Children's Friends*, 98–101.

"Her Spirit Apparently Left Her Body"
Woodruff, 52–55. Death of Sarah Emma: Morris, 10–11.

BIBLIOGRAPHY

Articles

Alexander, Thomas G. "Wilford Woodruff and Zion's Camp: Baptism by Fire and the Spiritual Confirmation of a Future Prophet." *BYU Studies* 39.1 (2000): 130–46.

Anderson, Richard L. "I Have a Question." *Ensign*, March 1979, 42–44.

Bennett, Richard E. "Elder Charles A. Callis: Twentieth-Century Missionary." *Ensign*, April 1981, 46–51.

Hall, David. "Anxiously Engaged: Amy Brown Lyman and Relief Society Charity Work, 1917–45." *Dialogue* 27 (Summer 1994): 73–91.

Jacobson, Marba C. "John A. Widtsoe—1872–1952." *Improvement Era*, January 1953, 18–19, 58–61.

Kimball, Edward L. "Harvey Fletcher and Henry Eyring: Men of Faith and Science." *Dialogue* 15 (Autumn 1982): 74–86.

———. "Science and Religion: A Dialogue with Henry Eyring." *Dialogue* 8 (Autumn/Winter, 1973): 100–8.

Madsen, Carol Cornwall. "A Bluestocking in Zion: The Literary Life of Emmeline B. Wells." *Dialogue* 16 (Spring 1983): 126–40.

Mangum, Dianne L. "The First Sister Missionaries." *Ensign*, July 1980, 62–65.

Rigdon, John Wickliffe. "The Life and Testimony of Sidney Rigdon." *Dialogue* 1 (Winter 1966): 18–42.

Rodriguez, Derin Head. "Flora Amussen Benson: Handmaiden of the Lord, Helpmeet of a Prophet, Mother in Zion." *Ensign*, March 1987, 14–20.

Todd, Jay M. "President Howard W. Hunter: Fourteenth President of the Church." *Ensign*, July 1994, 4–5.

Books

Allen, James B., and Glen M. Leonard. *The Story of the Latter-day Saints.* 1976. Salt Lake City: Deseret Book, 1992.

Anderson, Lavina Fielding, ed. *Lucy's Book: A Critical Edition of Lucy Mack Smith's Family Memoir.* Salt Lake City: Signature Books, 2001.

Andrus, Hyrum L., and Helen Mae Andrus. *They Knew the Prophet*. Salt Lake City: Bookcraft, 1974.

Arrington, Leonard J. *Brigham Young: American Moses*. Urbana and Chicago: University of Illinois Press, 1986.

Arrington, Leonard J., and Susan Arrington Madsen. *Mothers of the Prophets*. Salt Lake City: Deseret Book, 1987.

Bushman, Richard L. *Joseph Smith and the Beginnings of Mormonism*. Urbana and Chicago: University of Illinois Press, 1984.

Campbell, Eugene E., and Richard D. Poll. *Hugh B. Brown: His Life and Thought*. Salt Lake City: Bookcraft, 1975.

Cannon, Donald Q., and David J. Whittaker, eds. *Supporting Saints: Life Stories of Nineteenth-Century Mormons*. Provo, Utah: BYU Religious Studies Center, 1985.

Church History in the Fulness of Times: The History of The Church of Jesus Christ of Latter-day Saints. Prepared by the Church Educational System for Religion Courses 341–43. Salt Lake City: The Church of Jesus Christ of Latter-day Saints, 1989.

Clark, Ronald W. *Einstein: The Life and Times*. New York: World Publishing Company, 1971.

Conn, Peter. *Pearl S. Buck: A Cultural Biography*. New York: Cambridge University Press, 1996.

Cowley, Matthew. *Matthew Cowley Speaks*. Salt Lake City: Deseret Book, 1954.

Cowley, Matthias F. *Wilford Woodruff: History of His Life and Labors*. Salt Lake City: Deseret Book, 1901.

Derr, Jill Mulvay, Janath Russell Cannon, and Maureen Ursenbach Beecher. *Women of Covenant: The Story of Relief Society*. Salt Lake City: Deseret Book, 1992.

Deseret News 1999–2000 Church Almanac. Salt Lake City: The Church of Jesus Christ of Latter-day Saints, 1998.

Firmage, Edwin B., ed. *An Abundant Life: The Memoirs of Hugh B. Brown*. 2d ed., enlarged. Salt Lake City: Signature Books, 1999.

Flake, Lawrence R. *Prophets and Apostles of the Last Dispensation*. Provo, Utah: BYU Religious Studies Center, 2001.

Garr, Arnold, Donald Q. Cannon, and Richard O. Cowan. *Encyclopedia of Latter-day Saint History*. Salt Lake City: Deseret Book, 2000.

Gibbons, Francis M. *Dynamic Disciples, Prophets of God*. Salt Lake City: Deseret Book, 1996.

Goates, L. Brent. *Harold B. Lee: Prophet and Seer*. Salt Lake City: Bookcraft, 1985.

Hartshorn, Leon R, comp. *Remarkable Stories from the Lives of Latter-day Saint Women*. Salt Lake City: Deseret Book, 1973.

Herrmann, Dorothy. *Helen Keller: A Life*. New York: Alfred A. Knopf, 1998.

Hill, Donna. *Joseph Smith: The First Mormon*. Midvale, Utah: Signature Books, 1977.

Holzapfel, Richard Neitzel, and R. Q. Shupe. *Joseph F. Smith: Portrait of a Prophet*. Salt Lake City: Deseret Book, 2000.

Jenson, Andrew. *Latter-day Saint Biographical Encyclopedia: A Compilation of Biographical Sketches of Prominent Men and Women in The Church of Jesus Christ of Latter-day Saints*. 4 vols. Salt Lake City: A. Jenson History Company and Deseret News, 1901–1936.

Jesse, Dean C., ed. *The Papers of Joseph Smith, Volume I: Autobiographical and Historical Writings*. Salt Lake City: Deseret Book, 1989.

———. *The Papers of Joseph Smith, Volume II: Journal, 1832–1842*. Salt Lake City: Deseret Book, 1992.

———. *The Personal Writings of Joseph Smith*. Salt Lake City: Deseret Book, 1984.

Keller, Helen. *The Story of My Life*. Garden City, N.Y.: Doubleday, 1954.

Kimball, Edward L., and Andrew E. Kimball Jr. *Spencer W. Kimball: Twelfth President of The Church of Jesus Christ of Latter-day Saints*. Salt Lake City: Bookcraft, 1977.

Ludlow, Daniel H., ed. *Encyclopedia of Mormonism*. 4 vols. New York: Macmillan, 1992.

Lyman, Amy Brown. *In Retrospect: Autobiography of Amy Brown Lyman*. Salt Lake City: General Board of Relief Society, 1945.

Madsen, Carol Cornwall. *In Their Own Words: Women and the Story of Nauvoo*. Salt Lake City: Deseret Book, 1994.

Madsen, Carol Cornwall, and Mary E. Stovall. *As Women of Faith: Talks Selected from the BYU Women's Conferences*. Salt Lake City: Deseret Book, 1989.

Madsen, Truman G. *Defender of the Faith: The B. H. Roberts Story*. Salt Lake City: Bookcraft, 1994.

McKay, Llewelyn, comp. *Home Memories of President David O. McKay.* Salt Lake City: Deseret Book, 1956.

Middlemiss, Clare, comp. *Man May Know for Himself: Teachings of President David O. McKay.* Salt Lake City: Deseret Book, 1967.

Miner, Caroline Eyring, and Edward L. Kimball. *Camilla.* Salt Lake City: Deseret Book, 1980.

Morris, Larry E. *A Treasury of Latter-day Saint Letters.* Salt Lake City: Deseret Book, 2001.

Newell, Linda King, and Valeen Tippetts Avery. *Mormon Enigma: Emma Hale Smith.* Urbana and Chicago: University of Illinois Press, 1994.

O'Brien, Robert. Marriott: *The J. Willard Marriott Story.* Salt Lake City: Deseret Book, 1987.

Parry, Jay A., and Larry E. Morris. *The Mormon Book of Lists.* Salt Lake City: Bookcraft, 1987.

Peterson, Janet, and LaRene Gaunt. *The Children's Friends: Primary Presidents and Their Lives of Service.* Salt Lake City: Deseret Book, 1996.

————. *Elect Ladies.* Salt Lake City: Deseret Book, 1990.

Pusey, Merlo J. *Builders of the Kingdom: George A. Smith, John Henry Smith, George Albert Smith.* Provo, Utah: Brigham Young University Press, 1981.

Quinn, D. Michael. *J. Reuben Clark: The Church Years.* Provo, Utah: Brigham Young University Press, 1983.

Reese, W. L. *Dictionary of Philosophy and Religion.* Atlantic Highlands, N.J.: Humanities Press, 1980.

Richards, Claude. *J. Golden Kimball: The Story of a Unique Personality.* Salt Lake City: Deseret News Press, 1934.

Roberts. B. H. *A Comprehensive History of The Church of Jesus Christ of Latter-day Saints, Century One.* 6 vols. Salt Lake City: The Church of Jesus Christ of Latter-day Saints, 1930.

————. *The Life of John Taylor, Third President of The Church of Jesus Christ of Latter-day Saints.* Salt Lake City: George Q. Cannon & Sons, 1892.

Romney, Thomas C. *The Life of Lorenzo Snow, Fifth President of The Church of Jesus Christ of Latter-day Saints.* Salt Lake City: Sugarhouse Press, 1955.

Rudd, Glen L. *Pure Religion: The Story of Church Welfare Since 1930.* Salt Lake City: The Church of Jesus Christ of Latter-day Saints, 1995.

Smith, Barbara B., and Blythe Darlyn Thatcher, eds. *Heroines of the Restoration.* Salt Lake City: Bookcraft, 1997.

Smith, Henry A. *Matthew Cowley: Man of Faith*. Salt Lake City: Bookcraft, 1954.

Smith, Joseph. *History of The Church of Jesus Christ of Latter-day Saints*. Ed. B. H. Roberts. 7 vols. 2d ed. rev. Salt Lake City: Deseret Book, 1948.

Smith, Joseph Fielding. *Life of Joseph F. Smith*. Salt Lake City: Deseret Book, 1938.

Smith, Joseph Fielding Jr., and John J. Stewart. *The Life of Joseph Fielding Smith*. Salt Lake City: Deseret Book, 1972.

Snow, Eliza R. *Biography and Family Record of Lorenzo Snow*. Salt Lake City: Deseret News Company, 1884.

————. *An Immortal: Selected Writings of Eliza R. Snow*. N.p.: Nicholas G. Morgan, Sr., Foundation, 1957.

Staker, Susan, ed. *Waiting for World's End: The Diaries of Wilford Woodruff*. Salt Lake City: Signature Books, 1993.

Talmage, John R. *The Talmage Story: Life of James E. Talmage—Educator, Scientist, Apostle*. Salt Lake City: Bookcraft, 1972.

Tate, Lucile C. *LeGrand Richards, Beloved Apostle*. Salt Lake City: Bookcraft, 1982.

Taylor, Samuel W. *The Last Pioneer: John Taylor, a Mormon Prophet*. Salt Lake City: Signature Books, 1999.

Tullidge, Edward W. *The Women of Mormondom*. New York: Tullidge & Crandall, 1877.

Van Wagoner, Richard S., and Steven C. Walker. *A Book of Mormons*. Salt Lake City: Signature Books, 1982.

Vogel, Dan, ed. and comp. *Early Mormon Documents, Volume I*. Salt Lake City: Signature Books, 1996.

————. *Early Mormon Documents, Volume II*. Salt Lake City: Signature Books, 1998.

Whitney, Orson F. *Through Memory's Halls: The Life Story of Orson F. Whitney as Told by Himself*. Salt Lake City: Zion's Printing and Publishing Company, 1930.

Widtsoe, John A. *In a Sunlit Land: The Autobiography of John A. Widtsoe*. Salt Lake City: Deseret News Press, 1952.

Woodruff, Wilford. *Leaves from My Journal*. Salt Lake City: Juvenile Instructor Office, 1881.

INDEX OF KEY NAMES

INDEX OF KEY NAMES